ROMANS

by Ed Landry

A helpful guide through the greatest letter ever written in the history of the Church

AN EASY-TO-UNDERSTAND BIBLE COMMENTARY

Romans - An easy-to-understand Bible Commentary
#3 in the easy-to-understand Bible Commentary series
Copyright © 2019 by Uplifting Christian Books

Published in Nashville, TN by Uplifting Christian Books
All rights reserved.

Printed in the Philippines by SAM Printing Press
Printed in the USA by Kindle Direct Publishing

No part of this book may be reproduced in any written, electronic, recording, or photocopying without written permission of the publisher or author. The exception would be in the case of brief quotations embodied in the critical articles or reviews and pages where permission is specifically granted by the publisher or author.

Scriptures marked AMP are taken from the AMPLIFIED BIBLE (AMP): Scripture taken from the AMPLIFIED® BIBLE, Copyright © 1954, 1958, 1962, 1964, 1965, 1987 by the Lockman Foundation Used by Permission. (www.Lockman.org).

Scriptures marked HCSB are taken from the HOLMAN CHRISTIAN STANDARD BIBLE (HCSB): Scripture taken from the HOLMAN CHRISTIAN STANDARD BIBLE, copyright© 1999, 2000, 2002, 2003 by Holman Bible Publishers, Nashville Tennessee. All rights reserved.

Scriptures marked NLT are taken from the HOLY BIBLE, NEW LIVING TRANSLATION (NLT): Scriptures taken from the HOLY BIBLE, NEW LIVING TRANSLATION, Copyright© 1996, 2004, 2007 by Tyndale House Foundation. Used by permission of Tyndale House Publishers, Inc., Carol Stream, Illinois 60188. All rights reserved. Used by permission.

Scriptures marked KJV are taken from the KING JAMES VERSION (KJV): KING JAMES VERSION, public domain.

Scriptures marked NASB are taken from the NEW AMERICAN STANDARD (NAS): Scripture taken from the NEW AMERICAN STANDARD BIBLE®, copyright© 1960, 1962, 1963, 1968, 1971, 1972, 1973, 1975, 1977, 1995 by The Lockman Foundation. Used by permission.

Scriptures marked NIV are taken from the NEW INTERNATIONAL VERSION (NIV): Scripture taken from THE HOLY BIBLE, NEW INTERNATIONAL VERSION ®. Copyright© 1973, 1978, 1984, 2011 by Biblica, Inc.™. Used by permission of Zondervan.

Author - Ed Landry
Editorial team- Special thanks are due to John, OraLee, Janet, Herb, Marcia & Del.
Book and cover design by Ed and Janet Landry.
Illustrations by Ed Landry.
Development team, readers - The Thursday Group (David and Kathy, Janet, Larry and Patti, David K., Larry and Doreen, Lisa, Heidi, John, Joe, Rick and Nancy, Herb and Miraflor, Buddy and Marcia, and OraLee).

ISBN-13: 978-0-9990931-2-2

Printed in the United States of America.

D0218412

Dedication

This commentary on Paul's Epistle to the Romans is dedicated to the thousands of evangelical pastors and church planters laboring throughout the world. They have proven to be highly dedicated servants of Christ, many of whom endure great financial hardships, often lacking the basic ministry resources many in other countries consider essential. My prayer is that this book will bless you as you seek to communicate the way of salvation to your country.

May God richly bless you,
Your fellow servant,

Ed Landry
First Love International Ministries

Table of contents

Introduction

NOTE: THIS INTRODUCTION IS VERY HELPFUL TO UNDERSTAND THE CONTEXT OF THE EPISTLE TO THE ROMANS, PLEASE DON'T SKIP OVER IT.

Romans
THE STORY OF THE ENTIRE BIBLE

If you want one book to read that best summarizes the story of the entire Bible, it is Paul's Epistle to the Romans. It begins with the depth of human sin and bondage which results in the damaged creation of God. The journey takes us through an unimaginable rescue plan. Designed by our God of grace for all the catastrophic effects of the Fall of man.

That rescue takes place on the cross where the Lamb of God paid the complete penalty we deserved for our sin. He secured a full pardon from our guilt and issued an emancipation proclamation from sin's bondage. This provides us a secure home with the very God we have offended. The mercy and wisdom of our loving God is displayed as slaves to sin are set free from bondage. The entire cursed universe is given hope. Jews and Gentiles alike are reconciled to God. All mankind are welcomed into one forever family, Christ's Church.

The living, growing, body of Christ has been given a road map to avoid the temptations of the flesh and the pitfalls of a pagan society. It is a journey from the darkest dungeon to the brightest light of eternal day. **Welcome to Paul's Epistle to the Romans.**

MEET PAUL, THE AUTHOR

Other than Jesus Christ, no other person in history has had a greater impact on the Church and its growth than the Apostle Paul. He began his life as Saul, born and raised in an orthodox Jewish home in Tarsus (Southern Turkey today).

Paul's father was a Pharisee and Paul followed in his father's path. He grew in knowledge and influence within the Jewish culture and eventually became a powerful figure in the religious world. After the death and resurrection of Christ, Paul became an official defender of the Jewish religious/political system and the main persecutor of the followers of Jesus. He was responsible for the stoning of Steven **(Acts 7)**. Paul was a zealot for his Pharisee position and the honor of his Jewish heritage. He was a man feared by the Jewish believers. He was climbing the ladder of influence in society and religion.

But, God had a different plan!

> **"Now Saul, still breathing threats and murder against the disciples of the Lord, went to the high priest, ² and asked for letters from him to the synagogues at Damascus, so that if he found any belonging to the Way, both men and women, he might bring them bound to Jerusalem. ³ As he was traveling, it happened that he was approaching Damascus, and suddenly a light from heaven flashed around him; ⁴ and he fell to the ground and heard a voice saying to him, "Saul, Saul, why are you persecuting Me?" ⁵ And he said, "Who are You, Lord?" And He said, "I am Jesus whom you are persecuting, ⁶ but get up and enter the city, and it will be told you what you must do."** (Acts 9:1-6)

AND THE REST IS HISTORY

Saul, the persecutor of the Church became Paul, the planter of the church. From a detractor to a defender, an enemy became an evangelist, and from a hater of the Church to a hero of the faith. Yes, God had a different plan and what a plan it was. It would involve great trials, like a blacksmith hammering super-heated metal into a new shape. Paul would be melted, pounded and forged into a man of God. God said of him, "... he is a chosen instrument of Mine, to bear My name before the Gentiles and kings and the sons of Israel; **[16] for I will show him how much he must suffer for My name's sake.**" (Acts 9:15, 16).

Paul went on to plant churches all over Asia Minor, Macedonia, Achaia, and Greece. He wrote half of the New Testament. He changed the known world for Christ. Before Paul died at the hand of Nero, he left the church an inspired library of theology and Christian practice and in that library was the greatest single letter ever written in human history, the Epistle to the Romans.

THE EPISTLE TO THE ROMANS

We pick up this story at the end of the Apostle Paul's third missionary journey. After three years of ministry in Ephesus, the great Roman seaport in Asia minor, a major riot occurred and it was felt best for Paul to leave the city and so he did. He left his young disciple, Timothy, in charge of the Ephesian church.

> **"When the uproar had ended, Paul sent for the disciples and, after encouraging them, said goodbye and set out for Macedonia. [2] He traveled through that area, speaking many words of encouragement to the people, and finally arrived in Greece, [3] where he stayed three months."**
> (Acts 20:1-3)

His first time in Corinth, Paul had planted a significant, yet troubled church. He lived there 18 months working in partnership with others like Timothy, Silas, and Priscilla and Aquila. On this trip to

9

Corinth, Paul wrote the Epistle to the Romans and sent it to them with the help of an amazing lady who lived in the Corinthian eastern seaport village of Cenchrea. Her name was Phoebe **(Romans 16:1)**. Paul tells the Romans that he hopes to visit them on his way to Spain **(Rom 15:22-24)**. His former co-workers, Priscilla and Aquila, had already returned to their home city of Rome, and so he sends greetings to them and many other co-workers living in Rome who Paul longed to see again **(Romans 16)**.

The epistle Paul wrote to the Romans was not just a book of greeting. It was a masterpiece of instruction in theology and Christian living to the oppressed believers living in one of the most pagan societies on the earth. As it turned out, Paul apparently never did make it to Spain and his letter to the Church at Rome is known as his greatest and most comprehensive work.

PAUL'S FINAL LIFE CHAPTER

The Epistle to the Roman church had been written and sent off. It was the summer of AD 57. Paul then returned to Jerusalem where he would begin a season of trials and imprisonments that would end up sending him to Rome where he would live under house arrest in the city, yet free to minister. This is where the book of Acts ends. He was later released and returned to Greece and Macedonia to revisit the churches. Paul would later travel to Rome one last time where he, as tradition tells, would be beheaded by the evil emperor of the Roman Empire, Nero.

We actually get to read what those believers in Rome read. Try to imagine yourself back in that time and setting when you read it. To do that we need to understand what the Roman Empire was like.

A TOUR OF ANCIENT ROME

When the Apostle Paul walked the streets of Rome, it was the largest and most powerful city in the world. It was the capital of one of history's greatest and longest lasting empires ever. It lasted 1,500 years when you calculate all the forms it took over the years. Rome had 1.2 million inhabitants when the Apostle Paul was there. It was during a time of its greatest glory.

A FEW OF ROME'S NOTABLE ACHIEVEMENTS

ROMAN AQUEDUCTS. Rome was among the first civilizations to control and harness water's power. 1,000 cubic meters (260,000 US gallons) of water were brought into ancient Rome by 14 different aqueducts each day. Per capita, water usage in ancient Rome matched that of modern-day cities like New York City.

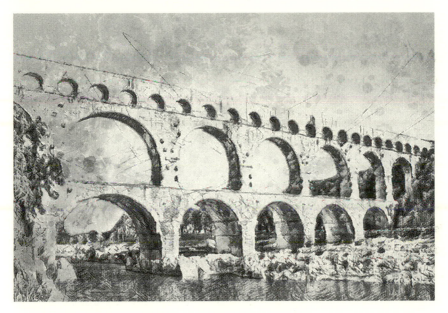

Roman engineers designed a system of reservoirs and elevated bridges and they used watermills to power grinding wheels for making flour.

ENGINEERING. Mining and crushing equipment were often run by hydraulic means. They forged great metal machines to extract ore. Their bridges and road systems are legendary and many can be seen today. They were designed to resist floods and other environmental hazards. The Romans invented concrete which alone has been a major factor in influencing our modern world. The Pantheon building can be seen in Rome today with its 130-foot diameter, poured-concrete dome ceiling. It was the largest concrete curved dome in existence until the nineteenth century. Much of the engineering was done by a well-trained military in order to advance the empire. They constructed forts, camps, bridges, roads, ramps, palisades, and siege equipment.

ARCHITECTURE. Roman design and construction were both beautiful and strong, enduring the test of time. Many structures use arches, domes and curves. The designs of ancient Rome have been a significant influence today in many large colosseums, government buildings, and cathedrals. They even invented central heating which spread all across Europe. They mined and manufactured their own building materials like brick, stone, masonry, cement, concrete and marble.

These are just glimpses into the impact the Roman Empire has had on the rest of the world. It was a very unique and advanced society. Along with all the scientific and engineering advances, there was a dark cancer eating away at the  great empire. We will look more at that when we study Romans chapter one. But first, let's finish the introduction to Rome during the first century, the Rome that Paul saw.

FUN AND UNUSUAL FACTS ABOUT ANCIENT ROME

- The first-ever shopping mall was built by Emperor Trajan in Rome. It consisted of several levels and more than 150 outlets that sold everything ranging from food and spices to clothing.
- Purple, the most expensive dye from Murex seashells, was reserved for the emperors' clothes or senators. It became treason for anyone other than the emperor to dress completely in purple.
- By the early fourth century, the Romans had built a road network of 53,000 miles throughout the empire. Each Roman mile was about 1,000 paces (about 4,800 feet) and was marked by a milestone.
- On the day the Colosseum officially opened, 5,000 animals were killed. During its history, over 500,000 people and over a million animals were killed there. The structure was built so efficiently that the exit time for all 70,000 spectators was only three minutes.
- The Circus Maximus could seat nearly 250,000 fans. It was the oldest and largest public space in Rome, originally laid out in the 6th century BC. Its principal function was as a chariot racetrack and host of the Roman Games (*early Olympics)*. Other events hosted at the site included wild animal hunts, public executions, and gladiator fights.

(From Fact Retriever, Karin Lehnardt)

WHAT LED TO THE FALL OF THE ROMAN EMPIRE?

Theories from historians abound as to why Rome fell.

- Political weakness
- Governmental corruption and internal fighting
- Widespread immorality
- Class conflict
- Environmental problems
- A divided capital (Rome and Constantinople)
- Plagues, and other outside influences

All of these existed. It was a complex set of problems and influences. Politicians see the basic problems as political. Environmentalists see it their way. As Christians, we see the entire Empire like a basket of rotten fruit. The moral decay and wide-spread sin infected all decisions, and ultimately the very foundations of the society collapsed. When immorality, lying, deception, human pride, and the worship of false gods is considered normal behavior, how can a society which mocks God continue to exist?

KEY VERSE IN ROMANS (If you could only pick one)

> **Romans 1:16–17 "For I am not ashamed of the gospel, for it is the power of God for salvation to everyone who believes, to the Jew first and also to the Greek. [17] For in it the righteousness of God is revealed from faith to faith; as it is written, "But the righteous man shall live by faith."**

UNIQUE FEATURES OF ROMANS

Romans quotes the Old Testament 74 times. Paul will deal with most of man's questions about God, man, sin, salvation, and our future hope. It will address most issues the church faces today. If you could read only one book in the entire Bible, then this would be the best pick.

Now, let's continue our journey into the incredible Epistle to the Romans. **Chapter One** will begin with why Paul wanted to go to Rome and then we will see the Gospel take center stage. The last half of the chapter will take us deep into the depraved society of the Roman Empire. It is indeed a journey into the dark side.

THE BIG QUESTIONS

How can a Christian live in a corrupt and depraved world like the Roman Empire? How do Christians live when all the world around them is worshiping false gods through immoral practices in heathen temples, and training their children to walk contrary to the Living God?

Romans Chapter 1
The Gospel is for both Jew and Gentile

16 "For I am not ashamed of the gospel, for it is the power of God for salvation to everyone who believes, to the Jew first and also to the Greek."

CHAPTER OVERVIEW

Romans One begins with Paul sending a greeting to the believers in ancient Rome, and also establishing himself as an Apostle, called by God, to the Gentile world. The Gospel, salvation, and the righteousness of God are primary themes which are firmly established and run throughout the entire Epistle. The last half of the chapter focuses on the depravity of the Roman Empire and the human race itself. The destructive avalanche of sin is described in vivid detail in complete contrast with the holiness and righteousness of our Creator.

KEY VERSES

[16] "For I am not ashamed of the gospel, for it is the power of God for salvation to everyone who believes, to the Jew first and also to the Greek. [17] For in it the righteousness of God is revealed from faith to faith; as it is written, 'BUT THE RIGHTEOUS man SHALL LIVE BY FAITH.'"

SIMPLE OUTLINE

I. **Paul's greeting, the Gospel, and the righteousness of God.** (1:1-17)

II. **Ancient Rome — A journey into the dark soul of fallen man.** (1:18-32)

Romans 1 Commentary

Romans 1:1-7 – Personal greeting and credentials as an apostle.

1 Paul, a bond-servant of Christ Jesus, called *as* an apostle, set apart for the gospel of God, **2** which He promised beforehand through His prophets in the holy Scriptures, **3** concerning His Son, who was born of a descendant of David according to the flesh, **4** who was declared the Son of God with power by the resurrection from the dead, according to the Spirit of holiness, Jesus Christ our Lord, **5** through whom we have received grace and apostleship to bring about *the* obedience of faith among all the Gentiles for His name's sake, **6** among whom you also are the called of Jesus Christ; **7** to all who are beloved of God in Rome, called *as* saints: Grace to you and peace from God our Father and the Lord Jesus Christ.

Romans 1:1-7, in many English versions, is one sentence. Paul often wrote complex sentences. For example, **Ephesians 1:3-14** is a single sentence in the Greek text. The Ephesians passage also contains 35 major doctrines. That is a lot to pack into a single sentence. Romans also has a complex beginning.

Paul mostly wrote to churches he had planted and to people he had discipled. But Paul had not yet been to Rome. At the time he wrote this epistle, Paul was actively engaged in dealing with the Judaizers, a growing movement to pull Christians back into the old Jewish system. It was an attack on the Gospel of grace and subverted believers into Jewish legalism. Paul makes certain in

Romans that grace is presented throughout and he warns and exposes the dangers of any attempt to be saved by human effort. His message to the Roman church in these opening verses was clear; the lost are saved by grace, made righteous by faith in God, and then all believers live by faith alone.

When a person is a slave to a system of self-righteousness, trying to keep the Law perfectly, in order to be accepted by God, it never leads to peace. A life like that is a constant struggle to be good enough for God. But when a person finds true peace with God, his struggle has ended. True peace only comes when our salvation is based on the finished work of Christ, not human effort. That is the peace Paul had found after a lifetime of futile works as a Pharisee. That is the reason Paul prays that the Romans will know that same grace of God and the true peace that comes from knowing Him **(v 7)**.

This introduction serves not just as an opening prayer of blessing on the Roman believers, but also as an introduction to Paul himself. Many had never met Paul but had heard about him. So, he gives his credentials. He was called out by God directly to be an Apostle. He was one of the privileged foundational individuals in the development of the Church. The Gospel Paul taught was the true Gospel. When Paul wrote to the Galatian church he had to rebuke them. They had left the true Gospel to follow a false gospel taught by the Judaizers **(Galatians 1)**. Paul begins Romans with authority because he has been set apart for the purpose of the true Gospel **(v 1)**. He reminds them that this true Gospel was promised in the Old Testament and fulfilled in the sending of God's Son, Jesus Christ. Christ fulfilled all that the prophets had predicted. He was the son of David and His death and resurrection was the declaration of God that He is the Savior, the Messiah **(vs 2-4)**.

The Gospel is for all, both Jew and Gentile people. Paul is

thrilled to be able to say to the Roman church that they too have found this peace with God. They are recipients of the grace of God because Christ has called them into the family of God. Even though Paul had not met many of the Roman believers, you can feel his joy that he is a kindred spirit with them as fellow members of the body of Christ. He passionately wants to see them face to face **(vs 5-7 and 11)**.

Paul's strong desire to see the believers in Rome

8 First, I thank my God through Jesus Christ for you all, because your faith is being proclaimed throughout the whole world. **9** For God, whom I serve in my spirit in the *preaching of the* gospel of His Son, is my witness *as to* how unceasingly I make mention of you, **10** always in my prayers making request, if perhaps now at last by the will of God I may succeed in coming to you. **11** For I long to see you so that I may impart some spiritual gift to you, that you may be established; **12** that is, that I may be encouraged together with you *while* among you, each of us by the other's faith, both yours and mine. **13** I do not want you to be unaware, brethren, that often I have planned to come to you (and have been prevented so far) so that I may obtain some fruit among you also, even as among the rest of the Gentiles. **14** I am under obligation both to Greeks and to barbarians, both to the wise and to the foolish. **15** So, for my part, I am eager to preach the gospel to you also who are in Rome.

Paul loved the church. He planted churches, discipled believers and always looked for Christians everywhere he went. He was especially drawn to the great cities which had influence in their regions. The greatest city in the world at that time was Rome but Paul had been unable to visit it even though he had made several attempts **(v 13)**.

The heart of Paul is revealed in these verses. He was thrilled that the testimony of the believers in Rome was impacting the Roman Empire **(v 8)**. Paul wanted to bless the church with his own gifts and to be mutually built up by the body of Christ in Rome **(v 11)**. He wanted them to know that he had tried to visit them but had been hindered. They were not forgotten and were being held up in the constant prayers of Paul **(vs 9,10)**.

The believers were under great stress by the intense spiritual warfare around them and persecutions that seemed endless. But it had produced in them a strong faith **(v 8)**. Paul wanted to make sure they had a clear understanding of the Gospel and its power to save all people **(v 14,15)**.

WHO ARE THE GREEKS, THE BARBARIANS, THE WISE AND UNWISE?

14 I am under obligation both to Greeks and to barbarians, both to the wise and to the foolish.

The Greeks

The powerful Roman empire grew out of the highly cultured Greek empire. The word "Greek" had become synonymous with "Gentiles" or non-Jews. The term "Greek", when used in the Roman empire, had a reputation for high culture, philosophy and worldly wisdom. Romans that spoke Greek were accepted as educated. It was the high class in Roman society.

The Barbarians

"Barbarians" referred to all non-Greeks. Specifically, if a Roman did not speak Greek, They were viewed as less cultured, even brutes. These Romans (Gentiles) were not viewed as "wise" like the educated Greeks. But to the Jews, all Gentiles, educated or otherwise, were considered as "dogs." **(Philippians 3:2, Matthew 15:21-28).**

The Wise and the Unwise or Foolish. This is a parallel reference to the Greeks and barbarians. "Wise" and "unwise" refer to cultured and uncultured. Paul wanted to spread the Gospel irrespective of ethnic or cultural background. There was no partiality in him.

THE MAIN PRINCIPLE OF THIS VERSE

God does not want us to distinguish between groups in giving the Gospel. The Gospel is the power of God bringing salvation to all who believe.

Even though Rome had the reputation of strongly persecuting Christians, Paul says he was eager to go there. The will of God and the direction of the Holy Spirit overshadowed any personal threat he might face in going to Rome. Paul wanted to make sure the Gospel was clearly understood and preached in that great city. Nothing was going to stand in the way. To Paul, it mattered not if a person was Jew, Greek, barbarian, wise or unwise, the Gospel was adequate to save.

Romans 1:16 and17 are the backbone of the entire Epistle. They are also a picture of the entire message of the Bible.

The Gospel

What is the Gospel?

The question "What is the Gospel?" is perhaps the most important question a person can ask. The word *Gospel* literally means "good news." It is the plan that God has designed to save sinful humans from eternal separation from Him.

What is the Gospel? The Bad News

In order to fully understand how good this news really is, we must first understand the bad news.

We are all sinners. The Bible presents a clear and consistent message that all people have sinned. **Romans 3:23** says, "For all have sinned and fall short of the glory of God." Sin means that we have missed the mark (the perfect standard) that God has set for us.

As a result of the fall in the Garden of Eden, every part of us has been corrupted by sin—our minds, emotions, flesh. We don't seek after God.

The penalty for sin is death. Romans 6:23 says, "For the wages of sin is death, but the gift of God is eternal life in

Christ Jesus our Lord." What is a wage? It is the "money that is paid or received for work or services." In other words, it is what you deserve, what you earn. **Romans 6:23** says that death is the wage for our sin. It is what we earn. We deserve to die and live separated from God forever.

What is the Gospel? The Good News

Since there is no way we can earn our way back to God, the Bible says He came to us! This is the good news—the Gospel.

Christ died for you. Romans 5:8 says, "But God demonstrates his own love for us in this: While we were still sinners, Christ [Jesus] died for us." The Bible says that even though we deserve the death penalty for our sin, Jesus took the penalty. He died in our place. Three days later, Jesus rose from death, proving that sin had been conquered.

You can be saved through faith in Christ. Ephesians 2:8-9 says, "For it is by grace you have been saved, through faith—and this not from yourselves, it is the gift of God—not by works, so that no one can boast."

Romans 1:16-19 - The KEY passage to Romans

16 For I am not ashamed of **the gospel**, for it is **the power of God for salvation** to **everyone who believes**, to the Jew first and also to the Greek. **17** For in it **the righteousness of God** is revealed from faith to **faith**; as it is written, "But the **righteous man** shall live by **faith**."**18** For the **wrath of God** is revealed from heaven against **all ungodliness and unrighteousness of men** who suppress the truth in unrighteousness, **19** because that which is known about God is evident within them; for God made it evident to them.

Look at the **bold words** and concepts in these four verses:

1. The righteousness of God – His nature.
2. Ungodliness, unrighteousness (sin) – the condition of man, the fallen creation of God.
3. Wrath of God against sin – His emotional response to sin and His holy justice.
4. The Gospel – the power of God to save.
5. Salvation available for everyone.
6. Faith, belief.
7. Sinful man made righteous.

This is not only the general message of Romans, **it is the story of the Bible, the history of God and man.**

Let's take those seven concepts found in this incredible passage and use them to explain the Gospel.

We know that all mankind is fallen and "none seeks after God" **(Romans 3:11)**. "There is none righteous, no, not one" **(Romans 3:10)**. Because we are unrighteous by nature and practice, we are not able to fix our sin problem and that is why God Himself solved the curse of sin. Only God has the power to save. Only He can provide salvation to our broken and fallen souls. Jesus' death on the cross paid the penalty for our sins completely; He bore our unrighteousness and His death made us righteous by faith. Now we, as saved sinners, have the righteousness of God put on our spiritual account. The wrath of God we deserved is over because Jesus bore the holy wrath of God in our place.

That is what this passage says about the Gospel.

Concerning the Wrath of God

"God's wrath is His holiness stirred into activity against sin." (A.W. Pink)

"He who believes in the Son has eternal life, but he who does not obey the Son will not see life, but the wrath of God abides on him." (John 3:36)

When Jesus died on the cross He bore the entire wrath of God that we deserved. We, who believe, will now never face the wrath of God. If any person rejects the loving offer of God to remove our sins, then they will face God's wrath, His holy justice.

The next section of Chapter One takes us into a very dark place. We see the heart of a man who chooses sin over salvation, darkness over light, death over life. The concept of sin is developed from **Romans 1:18** through **Chapter 3:20**. It is the most complete description of sin and the heart of man found in the Bible.

Sin and salvation are the focus of Romans 1:18-3:20.

In **Chapters 1-3** Paul goes back and forth between Jews and Gentiles when dealing with sin. The Gentiles have the creation of God and conscience to convict them of sin. The Jews have those things and much more. They have the privilege of their history with God, His Law and promises. They are held accountable for much more. Where much is given, much is required.

The Great Moral Landslide

Romans 1:18-32 begins with the fallen condition of Rome itself. When we understand the depth of their sin, we begin to see why Paul desired so strongly to be with them to encourage and build the believers up in Christ.

To help understand this next section of **Romans 1,** I suggest you imagine a great landslide. Landslides usually begin small, but soon are highly destructive events. What begins with a few stones and sticks tumbling down a slope quickly escalates into a thunderous slide of trees and boulders crashing down a mountain, destroying everything in its path. Sin is very much like that. However, unlike a landslide, which ends after crashing down a hillside, sin continues to start new landslides and unless God stops the slide, man's ruin will be complete and continue into a lost eternity. Sin is a reproducing evil.

> **"The deceptive fruit of an evil deed, Is that of new sin, it becomes the seed."** (Author unknown)

We can only imagine the burden Paul felt for the believers in the ungodly city of Rome. Paul was a Roman citizen who had traveled throughout Greece, Macedonia, Asia minor and Galatia. He had seen the pagan temples and the immoral practices of the hedonistic religious system that had infected the entire empire. Christians living in this evil world were confronted daily by that dark environment and intensive spiritual warfare. The capital city of the first century world of darkness was Rome. How bad was it really? The answer to his question is found in **verses 18-32**.

Sin will now be the focus of the rest of Chapter One, all of Chapter Two and much of Chapter Three. But the good news is that the light of salvation shines brightly over the kingdom of evil.

The Depravity of Man

The total depravity of man does not mean that man is as bad as he can possibly be. It means that no part of our being is untouched or unaffected by the corruption of sin. Sin has enslaved the total person. Man is not basically good but is desperately broken and apart from God's intervention he will remain in that helpless state. All of mankind is spiritually dead, deceived by the enemy, and doomed, facing the wrath of God **(Ephesians 2:1-3)**.

> **⁴ But God, being rich in mercy, because of His great love with which He loved us, ⁵ even when we were dead in our transgressions, made us alive together with Christ (by grace you have been saved), ⁶ and raised us up with Him, and seated us with Him in the heavenly places in Christ Jesus.** (Ephesians 2:4-6)

1:18-32 Rome's Moral Landslide
THE SOURCE OF THE MORAL SLIDE (1:18-23)

18 For the wrath of God is revealed from heaven against all ungodliness and unrighteousness of men who suppress the truth in unrighteousness, **19** because that which is known about God is evident within them; for God made it evident to them. **20** For since the creation of the world His invisible attributes, His eternal power, and divine nature, have been clearly seen, being understood through what has been made, so that they are without excuse. **21** For even though they knew God, they did not honor Him as God or give thanks, but they became futile in their speculations, and their foolish heart was darkened. **22** Professing to be wise, they became fools, **23** and exchanged the glory of the incorruptible God for an image in the form of corruptible man and of birds and four-footed animals and crawling creatures.

\

This revealing passage exposes the heart of mankind and shows us just how deceived we are as a race. Even though God has given mankind all the evidence needed to acknowledge our Creator, mankind persists in rejecting God and replacing him with gods of his own imagination and making.

> [2] **"I am the Lord your God . . .** [3] **"You shall have no other gods before Me. "You shall not make for yourself an idol, or any likeness of what is in heaven above or on the earth beneath or in the water under the earth.** [5] **You shall not worship them or serve them; for I, the Lord your God, am a jealous God,"** (highlights from Exodus 20:1-5)

God has provided all men everywhere evidence of His infinite, creative power and glory, by the creation itself. We have been given enough knowledge and reasoning power and we are in actual contact with our created world by sight, smell, hearing, taste, and touch. The fingerprints of God are everywhere.

Even without the printed words in front of them, all men have an awareness that "In the beginning, God created the heavens and the earth."

EVEN THE MOST PRIMITIVE AND ISOLATED CULTURES KNOW THAT GOD EXISTS

My missionary experience has shown that cultures all over the earth understand that there is an unseen world that affects our seen world. They know that a great God is behind it all but they often also believe that something that was done in the past has made Him go away. Yet, the wonder of God is built into every man whenever he looks into the night sky or watches the birth of a child.

19 because that which is known about God is evident within them; for God made it evident to them. **20** For since the creation of the world His invisible attributes, His eternal power and divine nature, have been clearly seen, being understood through what has been made, so that they are without excuse.

In **Romans Chapter 2** we will find that God has given man an additional evidence, a conscience which provides an invisible moral compass, his moral law. Even remote tribal people understand some things are right and others wrong. After generations of rejecting this moral compass, it is common to see these cultures have a confused moral code and even embrace killing and treachery as high values. When these cultures hear the Gospel and repent, they are restored to God's purpose for man and find a joyful life instead of living with fear and hate.

So between Creation (external evidence) and personal conscience (internal evidence), all men have enough evidence of God to acknowledge Him.

IDOLATRY IS SUBSTITUTING SOMETHING FOR GOD

What happens to a race of people when they reject God, the Creator, and make for themselves idols and false gods? **Romans 1:18-32** describes where that leads and that is what happened to the Roman Empire.

The first thing that happens is God is insulted when any man rejects His power and glory. They seek to worship the very things God has created. It is a mockery of the living God to worship dead idols of stone and wood. Since God is Holy and Just, His righteous reaction to sin is wrath.

> **18** For the wrath of God is revealed from heaven against all ungodliness and unrighteousness of men who suppress the truth in unrighteousness,

This passage emphasizes those who understand that God is the Creator, yet intentionally suppress or hide this fact and lead others astray into the darkness. This leads to a life of futility.

> **21** For even though they knew God, they did not honor Him as God or give thanks, but they became futile in their speculations, and their foolish heart was darkened.

Jesus gave a similar warning:

> **"Let them alone; they are blind guides of the blind. And if a blind man guides a blind man, both will fall into a pit."**
> (Matthew 15:14)

In the church, teachers are warned about the responsibility of leadership.

> **"Let not many of you become teachers, my brethren, knowing that as such we will incur a stricter judgment."**
> (James 3:1)

31

This text has a strong proclamation of the wrath of God particularly against those who knew God and decided that they could make their own gods. Many followed into the darkness of idolatry.

The next thing that happens in this moral landslide is that man becomes arrogant in his rejection of God. He then substitutes other objects of worship to replace the true God.

> **22** Professing to be wise, they became fools, **23** and exchanged the glory of the incorruptible God for an image in the form of corruptible man and of birds and four-footed animals and crawling creatures.

Idolatry represents the greatest of sins against God. It violates the first and greatest commandment of God:

> [2] **"I am the Lord your God, who brought you out of the land of Egypt, out of the house of slavery.**
> [3] **"You shall have no other gods before Me.**
> [4] **"You shall not make for yourself an idol, or any likeness of what is in heaven above or on the earth beneath or in the water under the earth.** [5] **You shall not worship them or serve them; for I, the Lord your God, am a jealous God, visiting the iniquity of the fathers on the children, on the third and the fourth generations of those who hate Me ..."**
> (Exodus 20:2-5)

Idolatry is not just a rejection of God, it is a willful mockery of God. All who do this are called fools.

Do you remember what we first learned about landslides? The further they travel the more destructive they become. They pick up more and more debris crashing down the mountain. This next passage describes the damage of sin. It gets worse and worse the further it goes. Notice the progression.

Another thing to notice is that the further it goes God stops restraining man and lets the landslide just tumble into the valley of Hell. It is a terrible day when someone tells God he wants nothing to do with Him.

The Extent of the Moral Slide (24-32)

24 Therefore God gave them over in the lusts of their hearts to impurity, so that their bodies would be dishonored among them. **25** For they exchanged the truth of God for a lie, and worshiped and served the creature rather than the Creator, who is blessed forever. Amen. **26** For this reason God gave them over to degrading passions; for their women exchanged the natural function for that which is unnatural, **27** and in the same way also the men abandoned the natural function of the woman and burned in their desire toward one another, men with men committing indecent acts and receiving in their own persons the due penalty of their error. **28** And just as they did not see fit to acknowledge God any longer, God gave them over to a depraved mind, to do those things which are not proper, **29** being filled with all unrighteousness, wickedness, greed, evil; full of envy, murder, strife, deceit, malice; *they are* gossips, **30** slanderers, haters of God, insolent, arrogant, boastful, inventors of evil, disobedient to parents, **31** without understanding, untrustworthy, unloving, unmerciful; **32** and although they know the ordinance of God, that those who practice such things are worthy of death, they not only do the same, but also give hearty approval to those who practice them.

One strong example of how a landslide will spawn new land-slides is found today in the "gay" or homosexual movement. God is very clear, in both the New Testament and the Old Testament, to denounce the sin of homosexuality as a defiant immoral sin against God. God created marriage and sexual union as a gift to mankind, and He uses it to portray the union of Christ and the Church. Any union outside of God's creative purpose is called unnatural and sinful. Homosexual activity is clearly labeled as such, unnatural and sinful, and a mockery of God's creative purpose.

Today we see a strong, thundering landslide in the world. Homosexual marriages are, not just condoned, but promoted by various sectors of society and even governments. What has been, in the past, something not even spoken about in secret, is now, "out of the closet" and being celebrated. The landslide is gathering momentum and destroying many lives.

The Roman empire was a land of idolatry and immoral practices in the worship of their idols of wood and stone. Homosexuality was widespread in the empire; some historians say most of the Emperors of the Roman Empire were homosexual. The moral collapse was a strong contributing factor to the total collapse of the Empire.

THE PROGRESSION OF SIN SEEN IN ROMANS 1:18-32
Let's review what happened

(Vs. 24, 25) Idolatry begins the slide. The Creator has been replaced with idols. Man has said he doesn't need God, he can do it his own way. With God's loving restraint lifted, the heart of man becomes submerged into the swamp of sin.

(Vs. 26, 27) Sexual immorality spreads without love or conscience. It goes from excess to perversion. Homosexuality becomes widespread like in Sodom.

(Vs. 28-31) God gives the people over to depraved minds filled with all manner of evil. The slide increases with people abandoning the true God, violating the first and greatest commandment. Then they violate the second commandment by hating each other. Like rabid dogs, they turn on everyone. Twenty-one distinct, hateful and destructive sins are listed in these few verses. Sin had become their way of life. The danger is that when sin becomes a pattern it is viewed as normal, an accepted way of life.

(V. 32) The sin of the land became the accepted norm of society. In **verse 32** we see described a condition when a man knows he is doing is evil and heading toward a final day of reckoning with God, but he simply does not care. Then he promotes that evil behavior in others.

The Roman Empire became a massive moral landslide which affected all parts of society. In the end, it rotted from the inside. Paul was very blunt and descriptive that the sins he lists are not to be named among the people of God.

He gave the same warning to the believers in the Roman city of Ephesus. He also associated fleshly sins with idolatry.

> [3] **"But immorality or any impurity or greed must not even be named among you, as is proper among saints; [4] and there must be no filthiness and silly talk, or coarse jesting, which are not fitting, but rather giving of thanks. [5] For this you know with certainty, that no immoral or impure person or covetous man, who is an idolater, has an inheritance in the kingdom of Christ and God."** (Ephesians 5:3-5)

Chapters 2 and 3 continue the warnings concerning sin in the world. Paul addresses both Jews and Gentiles.

Romans Chapter 2
God impartially judges sin

CHAPTER OVERVIEW

The horror of sin was described in **1:18-32**. We now come to what could be called Sin 2.0, to use modern technical language. The first 16 verses show that God, who is holy, must judge sin. He does it impartially. **Chapter 2** is a continuation from **Chapter 1**, the heathen gentile nations. But in **2:17**, the focus goes to the Jewish nation who have put their trust in the keeping of the Law, rituals, and circumcision. Paul is clear. Without faith in God, and faith alone, no human effort will save a person. Without faith, Jews and Gentiles alike stand condemned.

KEY VERSES

[9]"There will be tribulation and distress for every soul of man who does evil, of the Jew first and also of the Greek, [10] but glory and honor and peace to everyone who does good, to the Jew first and also to the Greek. [11] For there is no partiality with God."

SIMPLE OUTLINE

I. Warning about passing judgment on others. (2:1-4)

II. God will impartially judge sin and reward what is good. (2:5-11)

III. Faith and works go hand in hand. (2:12-16)

IV. A special warning to the Jewish believers. (2:17-29)

Romans 2 Commentary

Warning about passing judgment on others (2:1-4)

1 Therefore you have no excuse, every one of you who passes judgment, for in that which you judge another, you condemn yourself; for you who judge practice the same things. **2** And we know that the judgment of God rightly falls upon those who practice such things. **3** But do you suppose this, O man, when you pass judgment on those who practice such things and do the same *yourself*, that you will escape the judgment of God? **4** Or do you think lightly of the riches of His kindness and tolerance and patience, not knowing that the kindness of God leads you to repentance?

This chapter begins with the word "therefore" so the message is clearly tied to the previous chapter. Paul is writing to the Church, made up of both Jewish and Gentile believers. Chapter One ended with a strong condemnation of sin and described the magnitude of the offense against God that was found in the Roman Empire. In **Romans 2:1**, he warns the Church about being judgmental or feeling superior to the wicked heathen. If it wasn't for the grace of God, everyone reading Paul's letter would be living in the same sin. No one has a right to be arrogant or boastful.

It is hard to tell who the "therefore" in **verse 1** is addressing. Some think it refers to the heathen Gentiles previously addressed. Others think it is the leaders of the Roman Empire. It might also be the now-saved Gentile members of the Church who, having been delivered from great sin, now look with disdain at the culture of sin around them. Most commentators believe that this warning by Paul was specifically to the Jewish believers in the Church who still struggled with arrogance and being judgmental.

The probable answer is that Paul was warning the entire Church to the dangers of personal arrogance and judgmental-ism. Many of the Church in Rome had been saved out of the disgusting life of sin Paul describes in **1:18-32**. They knew, according to **verse 2**, that God's judgment on that sin was rightly deserved. What they didn't understand, was that being judgmental was also sin. God would hold them accountable.

One principle is clear. Where much is given, much is required. Both Jew and Gentile believers had been delivered from great sin, given great grace. Neither had any grounds to point their fingers at those around them still trapped in sin.

All of us today need to be mindful of this very same thing. We see clearly the sins of others but are often blind to our own. We need to remember the very thing Paul was trying to impress on the church in Rome. Our repentance and salvation are a work of God **(2:4).** It was because of the kindness and patience of God, not because we deserved it. If there is anything to boast about, it is in God alone.

God will impartially judge sin and reward what is good (2:5-11)

5 But because of your stubbornness and unrepentant heart you are storing up wrath for yourself in the day of wrath and revelation of the righteous judgment of God, **6** who WILL RENDER TO EACH PERSON ACCORDING TO HIS DEEDS: **7** to those who by perseverance in doing good seek for glory and honor and immortality, eternal life; **8** but to those who are selfishly ambitious and do not obey the truth, but obey unrighteousness, wrath and indignation. **9** *There will be* tribulation and distress for every soul of man who does evil, of the Jew first and also of the Greek, **10** but glory and honor and peace to everyone who does good, to the Jew first and also to the Greek. **11** For there is no partiality with God.

These verses can be summed up by saying that God rewards all the good that believers do and punishes all evil with complete impartiality. It is just a fact based on His infinite and perfect justice, righteousness, love, and grace.

Verse 6 is an Old Testament quotation found in two places, **Psalm 62:12** and **Proverbs 24:12**. The concept of reaping what we sow is found throughout Scripture. It is both assuring for the believer and concerning for the guilty sinner that a final accounting will indeed take place. God will settle all the books, He will finish the story. He will "render to each person according to his deeds." It will be true, just and fair. To some, it means eternal life **(2:7)** and others wrath and indignation **(2:8).**

Chapter One proclaimed the Gospel as the power of God unto salvation to the Jew first and then the Greek. That is historically how the Gospel went forth. The nation of Israel received a special assignment to be the custodians of the message of salvation which was to bless all nations. Much was given to them and therefore much is required also. They are the first ones mentioned in verse nine when God brings distress and tribulation to all evildoers. Israel had the message first and were commanded to take it to others. They would be the first to face God for their failures. For those Jews who have shown faith in God doing what He called them to do, are the first rewarded **(v. 9).** God will also judge and reward the Greeks according to His impartial standards.

Faith and works go hand in hand (2:12-16)

12 For all who have sinned without the Law will also perish without the Law, and all who have sinned under the Law will be judged by the Law; **13** for *it is* not the hearers of the Law *who* are just before God, but the doers of the Law will be justified. **14** For when Gentiles who do not have the Law do instinctively the things of the Law, these, not having the Law, are a law to themselves, **15** in that they show the work of the Law written in their hearts, their conscience bearing witness and their thoughts alternately accusing or else defending them, **16** on the day when, according to my gospel, God will judge the secrets of men through Christ Jesus.

Chapter One described all mankind as being accountable to God because He has made sure He has made himself known to all men by the creation. Not only His existence but the creation broadcasts His Divine nature and power.

"¹⁹ "because that which is known about God is evident within them; for God made it evident to them. ²⁰ For since the creation of the world His invisible attributes, His eternal power and divine nature, have been clearly seen, being understood through what has been made, so that they are without excuse. ²¹ For even though they knew God, they did not honor Him as God or give thanks, but

they became futile in their speculations, and their foolish heart was darkened."
(Romans 1:19-21)

This is a description of a people that sinned without the Law. They will be held accountable for the knowledge of God that He has made known to them. In addition to that general revelation that God has given to every man, there is also the internal witness of His Goodness by the moral conscience God has placed within every man:

> [14] **"For when Gentiles who do not have the Law do instinctively the things of the Law, these, not having the Law, are a law to themselves,"**

Creation and human conscience are like built-in guiding lights in the soul of every person on the planet. Sin drives people to make idols of every kind. Anything that dethrones God and replaces Him with something from the dark imagination of man. What a person chooses to believe affects all his actions or deeds. As a man thinks in his heart, so is he **(Proverbs 23:7).** Faith and works go hand in hand. Works, or deeds, are the evidence of what a person believes. A man who builds idols and worships them does not have saving faith.

This is what **Romans 2:13-16** is talking about. Judgment will be based on what a man does, not what he says he believes. Jews who claim to follow the Law but don't have the good works that come through a true faith will be judged by the very Law they claim to follow. The heathen who don't have the Law, have the Law in their hearts and will be judged on their deeds, or as this passage hints, defended by their deeds. We may not know exactly what this phrase means, but we do know the Judge of the earth will do what is right. Here is the description God gives of that final impartial judgment:

11 "Then I saw a great white throne and Him who sat upon it, from whose presence earth and heaven fled away, and no place was found for them. **12** And I saw the dead, the great and the small, standing before the throne, and books were opened; and another book was opened, which is the book of life; and the dead were judged from the things which were written in the books, according to their deeds. **13** And the sea gave up the dead which were in it, and death and Hades gave up the dead which were in them; and they were judged, every one of them according to their deeds." (Revelation 20:11-13)

James talked about people that professed to believe in Christ but did not have the evidence in their lives that they were truly children of God. The evidence he was talking about was the good works a believer does after he becomes a Christian. These are works that come from his changed heart. They prove he is a Christian. Faith without these works is dead.
 (James Chapter 2)

When you combine **Ephesians 2:8-10** with **James 2** you get something like this:

Faith alone saves, but
The Faith that saves is never alone.

Paul will now sharpen the focus on the fact that Israel had built their eternal hopes on several false hopes. They had trusted in their heritage, their traditions, their good works and all the wrong things and had missed the simple way, the way of faith. Let's begin this next section with a brief look back at the nation of Israel as God's chosen people.

ISRAEL, THE CHOSEN PEOPLE OF GOD

God chose a specific people to be the channel to introduce the Messiah to the world. He could have chosen any race or nation to be the human family line through which the Savior of the world would come. God, the Son, became flesh, and for that to happen He had to be born through a family line. That line was the family of Abraham, Isaac and Jacob. Why did He pick the Jewish people? Were they better than other people?

Actually, all we know from Scripture is that God is sovereign. He chooses whom He chooses. He raises up and He pulls down. He is God. He makes the decisions based on His perfect knowledge. This is the choice He made. He loved Israel. He blessed them with the Law, the Temple, the privileges of a great heritage and many other blessings. God traveled with them through the desert, the new land He had given them, and through the centuries. They were protected and blessed in every way. They also faced the strong discipline of God when they wandered off His assigned path.

Many in Israel rejected their God. The Lord sent prophets to act as signposts to show them the way back.

Some of the Jews were boastful and arrogant because of the special affection God had shown the nation, and they lost sight of the privileges and responsibilities God had given them. They were supposed to be a light to the Gentile nations but failed many times. God has never forgotten His people. Romans contains many sections which deal directly with Israel. Paul answers several complaints and questions they had and seeks to bring them back to the God of their fathers. In the end, a believing remnant of Israel will be joined with believing Gentiles to form the completed church, the body of Christ.

A SPECIAL WARNING TO THE JEWISH BELIEVERS (2:17-29)

The first set of warnings were general in nature, dealing with works as a whole, and faith. It was also given to impress on both Jew and Gentile that God is impartial and fair. Now, because of the special privileges that were given to Israel, Paul wants to make sure they understand that these privileges are not what gets them to heaven. This is a topic close to the heart of Paul. He spent the first part of his life trusting in his heritage, his works and following the Law. In the end, it did not save him. He wants his people Israel to understand that these things are not what leads to eternal life.

The Law, the promises to Abraham, the covenants, the Temple, its services, priests, and feasts were all amazing ways that God explained the way of salvation based on faith. Without true faith, these privileges just became a system of dead works. Man used these to try to earn his way into Heaven.

FALSE HOPES

In this next section, Paul addresses the false hope of trusting in
45

a person's heritage and their "good works." The final thing he addresses is the false hope of trusting in one's circumcision.

There is a section of the Gospel of John which describes these three false hopes. Let's look at that first. We will see it serves as a perfect introduction to **Romans 2:17-29**.

> [10] **He was in the world, and the world was made through Him, and the world did not know Him.** [11] **He came to His own, and those who were His own did not receive Him.** [12] **But as many as received Him, to them He gave the right to become children of God, even to those who believe in His name, 13 who were born, not of blood nor of the will of the flesh nor of the will of man, but of God.**
> (John 1:10-13)

The Apostle John lists three births that will never get anyone to Heaven and then one birth that will.

Born of blood. Just because a person has a certain family line or heritage does not make them a believer. Many have families that have been members of a certain church for generations and may have been pillars in the church, but God only has children, not grandchildren. No one becomes a Christian based on their family line, no matter how wonderful that family. Many Jews could proudly name their tribal background and family history but that is not what makes a person right with God. This birth would be the false hope of trusting in one's heritage.

Born of the will of the flesh. Some base their hope on personal efforts, human works. Several Biblical passages are clear that salvation is by faith alone, not by works. Human effort will only give false hope. Salvation is a work of God, not based on the efforts of man.

Born of the will of man. Some base their salvation on what others have done for them. They have been baptized, circumcised, confirmed, blessed by some priest or some other thing done by someone else. An example would be the false hope for the Jew of trusting in their circumcision.

The one birth that makes the eternal difference is when a person is **Born of God.** This is the spiritual birth that puts us in the family of God. That birth comes by faith in the finished work of Christ and cannot be duplicated by any works of the flesh.

With those truths in mind let's look at **Romans 2:17-29.**

The false hope of trusting in heritage and works (2:17-24)

17 But if you bear the name "Jew" and rely upon the Law and boast in God, **18** and know *His* will and approve the things that are essential, being instructed out of the Law, **19** and are confident that you yourself are a guide to the blind, a light to those who are in darkness, **20** a corrector of the foolish, a teacher of the immature, having in the Law the embodiment of knowledge and of the truth, **21** you, therefore, who teach another, do you not teach yourself? You who preach that one shall not steal, do you steal? **22** You who say that one should not commit adultery, do you commit adultery? You who abhor idols, do you rob temples? **23** You who boast in the Law, through your breaking the Law, do you dishonor God? **24** For "THE NAME OF GOD IS BLASPHEMED AMONG THE GENTILES BECAUSE OF YOU,"

We see in this section how powerless the religion of the nation of Israel had become. God had given His chosen people so much. They had the law of God, the way of salvation so beautifully pictured in the priests, sacrifices, feasts and the Temple. They had the great heritage of Abraham, Isaac and Jacob and the covenants with the God of the universe. No people on earth had this except Israel. All Israel needed was faith. God wanted them to believe Him. Instead, they turned the gifts God had given them into a system of works which became a dead religion with empty practices. Jesus rebuked the leaders of Israel that they had become like whitewashed tombs, pretty on the outside but full of dead men's bones and all uncleanness on the inside **(Matthew 23:27).**

What God wanted was a relationship with His people. They wanted a religion with rules they could follow. They wanted a list so they could check off the boxes. What happened? They got just that, but without God. There was no power to live. The very laws they preached, they did not follow. It became so bad that the Gentile nations looking on saw the hypocrisy and mocked God because of the lives of the Jews **(2:24)**.

Verse 24 is a quote from **Isaiah 52:5**. The ungodly nations saw the failures and hypocrisy of Israel and used it as an excuse to sin more. After all, if the people of God can't follow the rules, why should they? Likewise, our lives, are on display day and night before the world. How we live before them preaches a stronger message than the words we speak.

When we get to **Romans 11,** we will see that a day is coming when all of true Israel will find their Messiah. God has not forgotten His people even though many have forgotten Him.

Paul rebuked the Jewish nation for having a form of godliness but without the power. They preached the moral law to others, but they failed to keep it. They trusted in their Jewish heritage **(2:17-20)** and in their works **(2:21-24),** but as we have seen in **John 1:13**, these things will not save a person.

The false hope of trusting in circumcision (2:25-29)

25 For indeed circumcision is of value if you practice the Law; but if you are a transgressor of the Law, your circumcision has become uncircumcision. **26** So if the uncircumcised man keeps the requirements of the Law, will not his uncircumcision be regarded as circumcision? **27** And he who is physically uncircumcised, if he keeps the Law, will he not judge you who though having the letter *of the Law* and circumcision are a transgressor of the Law? **28** For he is not a Jew who is one outwardly, nor is circumcision that which is outward in the flesh. **29** But he is a Jew who is one inwardly; and circumcision is that which is of the heart, by the Spirit, not by the letter; and his praise is not from men, but from God.

Let's begin by first understanding the reason behind circumcision.

- Have you ever wondered why God commanded His people Israel to be circumcised?

- Why this particular operation on that part of the male anatomy?

Circumcision
CIRCUMCISION. WHY DID GOD REQUIRE SUCH A THING?

It all began with a big problem!

> "Therefore, just as through one man sin entered into the world, and death through sin, and so death spread to all men, because all sinned." (Romans 5:12)

Sin entered the human race and only God could solve it. The solution was almost unthinkable. The eternal God would enter the human race and become the sacrifice for the sin of man. God the Son would become the slaughtered sacrificial lamb. God would become flesh.

> **"And the Word (Christ) became flesh, and dwelt among us, and we saw His glory, glory as of the only begotten from the Father, full of grace and truth."**
> (John 1:14)

GOD CHOSE A PEOPLE FOR A VERY SPECIAL ROLE.

For God to enter the human race, He had to choose a human family line. Why did he choose the line of Shem (the Semitic people)? We are not told. God is sovereign, and He made the call. It wasn't that they were better, or more faithful, or anything else. They were God's choice. God the Son had a family line. The entire Old Testament focuses on that family and points to the One who is coming that will be the Savior of the world. Adam brought sin and death into the world and Christ would bring forgiveness and life in its place.

> **For as in Adam all die, so also in Christ all will be made alive.**
> (1 Corinthians 15:22)

GOD CHOSE A SPECIAL MAN FOR A VERY SPECIAL TASK

> [1] **"Now when Abram was ninety-nine years old, the LORD appeared to Abram and said to him,"**

THE COVENANT GOD MADE WITH ABRAHAM

> **"I am God Almighty;**
> **Walk before Me, and be blameless.**
> [2] **"I will establish My covenant between Me and you,**
> **And I will multiply you exceedingly."**
> [3] **Abram fell on his face, and God talked with him, saying,**

50

[4] "As for Me, behold, My covenant is with you,
And you will be the father of a multitude of nations.
[5] "No longer shall your name be called Abram,
But your name shall be Abraham;
For I have made you the father of a multitude of nations.
[6] I will make you exceedingly fruitful, and I will make
nations of you, and kings will come forth from you. [7] I
will establish My covenant between Me and you and your
descendants after you throughout their generations for
an everlasting covenant, to be God to you and to your
descendants after you. [8] I will give to you and to your descendants after you, the land of your sojournings, all the
land of Canaan, for an everlasting possession; and I will be
their God."

CIRCUMCISION - THE SIGN OF THE COVENANT WITH ABRAHAM

[9] "God said further to Abraham, "Now as for you, you shall
keep My covenant, you and your descendants after you
throughout their generations. [10] This is My covenant,
which you shall keep, between Me and you and your
descendants after you: every male among you shall be
circumcised. [11] And you shall be circumcised in the flesh
of your foreskin, and it shall be the sign of the covenant
between Me and you." (Genesis 17:1-11)

BUT WHY CIRCUMCISION?

Abraham was to father a nation. His children and all that followed were to carry with them a constant reminder in their
own bodies of their God-assigned family line. Every male bore
the sign of the covenant and that sign was a part of every intimate act that produced the chosen line. They were the people
that God used to bring the Messiah into the world. Although it
was a physical sign, it also was a spiritual covenant, a heart ded-
ication of faithfulness to the Living God. It is the heart condition
that **Romans 2** is addressing. A circumcised body without a
circumcised heart is just dead religion.

Now let's look at the passage in **Romans 2:25-29**. As beautiful as the covenant was, and the intimacy contained in the sign of the covenant, circumcision, like other parts of the Jewish religious system, soon became a source of pride as a race. It was meant to be a reminder of a special relationship and responsibility for Israel to live lives worthy of the God who had chosen them for such a sacred task.

Sadly, for some, it was seen as a ticket to Heaven, a guaranteed seat with Abraham at the great feast of God in eternity. It would be the same if you asked a Christian today how he knew he was saved, and he said he was certain of eternal life because he had been baptized. Personally, as a child, I was baptized, but I became a Christian in my early 20's when, by faith, I trusted Christ to be my Savior. As a child I trusted in my baptism for much of my early life. It was a false hope, just as when a Jewish person trusts in circumcision to make them a part of the family of God.

CIRCUMCISION OF THE HEART VERSUS THE FLESH

Romans 2:27-29 is a very important section of Romans. The main lesson of this passage is that there are actually two types of people who belong to the Jewish nation. There are Jews that are of the flesh and there are those of the Spirit.

Those of the flesh are the ones raised in the heritage of the Jewish customs. They had been circumcised, kept the festivals and traditions of the nation. These things were not bad things, they were instituted by God. The missing piece, however, is faith in God, a true heartfelt commitment to the God of Israel. They are described in this passage as circumcised in the flesh. They are of the flesh, an outward show, a religious exercise. Their heart is not in it. There is no actual personal faith. They have all the wonderful heritage and privilege given to Israel, but they are dead to God. They live out a hollow religious system based on human effort. Their bodies have been circumcised, but their hearts have not. It is all flesh, not Spirit-controlled.

The second group are the real believers. They have a physical circumcision as well. The difference is that this group is not just going through the motions, doing their religious thing, these are genuine believers in God. They have the Spirit of God because of faith. They are referred to as true Israel. They are also referred to in both the Old Testament and New Testament as the "Remnant." They are the smaller number making up the Jewish nation. They are the true children of God in that community. This will be very important to keep in mind when we get to **Chapters 9-11** of Romans. These true believers, circumcised in the heart, the Remnant, are the ones that will be saved in the end. They are true Israel.

Summary of Chapters 1 and 2

The Gentile world with their heathen practices is lost. They need salvation which can only come through faith in Christ.

The Jewish world with it's Law, circumcision, and temple worship is dead as a whole because they trust in their religion instead of the living God. They need salvation which can only come through faith in Christ.

Chapter 3 will pick it up from there and continue the same themes. Paul is laying out a strong systematic argument about the nature and extent of sin in all the human race. This is a critical foundation to build upon as he presents the work of Christ and the great hope of salvation for all people.

Romans 3

"All have sinned and fall short of the glory of God"

Romans 3:23

CHAPTER OVERVIEW

Paul concludes the convincing presentation he started in **Chapter 1**. Both Jews and Gentiles are equally guilty before God. All have sinned and fall short of the glory of God **(3:23)**. Whether they have the Law of God written in stone or in their hearts, all men are guilty before God. The good news is that there is a pardon available to all, given by God, the Righteous Judge.

KEY VERSES FOR CHAPTER 3

> [21] "But now apart from the Law the righteousness of God has been manifested, being witnessed by the Law and the Prophets, [22] even the righteousness of God through faith in Jesus Christ for all those who believe; for there is no distinction; [23] for all have sinned and fall short of the glory of God, [24] being justified as a gift by His grace through the redemption which is in Christ Jesus;"

SIMPLE OUTLINE

I. God is true and faithful in spite of the sins of Israel. (3:1-8)

II. All the world is guilty before God. (3:9-18)

III. Justification by faith. Light in the darkness. (3:19-31)

Romans 3 Commentary

God is true and faithful in spite of the sins of Israel (3:1-8)

1 Then what advantage has the Jew? Or what is the benefit of circumcision? **2** Great in every respect. First of all, that they were entrusted with the oracles of God. **3** What then? If some did not believe, their unbelief will not nullify the faithfulness of God, will it? **4** May it never be! Rather, let God be found true, though every man *be found* a liar, as it is written,

> "THAT YOU MAY BE JUSTIFIED IN YOUR WORDS,
> AND PREVAIL WHEN YOU ARE JUDGED."

5 But if our unrighteousness demonstrates the righteousness of God, what shall we say? The God who inflicts wrath is not unrighteous, is He? (I am speaking in human terms.) **6** May it never be! For otherwise, how will God judge the world? **7** But if through my lie the truth of God abounded to His glory, why am I also still being judged as a sinner? **8** And why not *say* (as we are slanderously reported and as some claim that we say), "Let us do evil that good may come"? Their condemnation is just.

When you read these eight verses and compare them with the last half of **Chapter 2,** it becomes clear that many in the Jewish nation had complaints against God. When we get to **Chapter 9** we will see that Paul basically spends the entire chapter (and part of **Chapter 10**) dealing with three complaints they had against God.

In **Chapter 9** the three complaints we will examine later are:

- **The Word of God has failed** so why should we trust God?
- **God is unfair, unjust** in the way He has treated us.
- If God is sovereign in His ways, then He has chosen our path ahead of time. Therefore, **we are not responsible for our own actions.** God is responsible.

In **Chapter 2** the rebukes he gives to Israel are in response to their complaints and attitudes which sounded like this:

What have we done wrong? We are children of Abraham. We have the Law of Moses and we keep it. We follow the priests and temple practices. We offer animals for our sins. We have been circumcised according to the command of God. What more can be expected of us? (The answer, of course, is faith.)

In **Chapter 3** here are their basic issues with God:

- If you show mercy to the sinful Gentiles who don't follow the Law and are not your chosen, special people, then what is the value of being a Jew. Why do we have so many requirements and they don't? What is fair in this?

- If my sins make grace abound and my lies and dishonesty result in God being seen as more holy and righteous, isn't that a good thing? Since we bring honor to God by being human, why should we be in danger of the wrath of God?

The final answer to all these complaints and challenges to the righteousness and fairness of God will be summarized later in **Chapter 9** when God says to His stubborn, complaining people:

¹⁹ You will say to me then, "Why does He still find fault? For who resists His will?" ²⁰ On the contrary, who are you, O man, who answers back to God? The thing molded will not say to the molder, "Why did you make me like this," will it? ²¹ Or does not the potter have a right over the clay, to make from the same lump one vessel for honorable use and another for common use? ²² What if God, although willing to demonstrate His wrath and to make His power known, endured with much patience vessels of wrath prepared for destruction? ²³ And *He did so* to make known the riches of His glory upon vessels of mercy, which He prepared beforehand for glory . . ." (Romans 9:19-23)

God needed to remind His people just who they were talking against. Just because we mortal people can't understand all the ways of God is not proof that God is at fault, is unfair, unloving or unrighteous. No, those things describe us, not God. God is patient and consistent in all His attributes. The one thing He wants from us is to trust Him. In other words, believe He is right even when we can't understand His ways. Every one of Israel's complaints could be answered by just believing God.

Let's briefly look at each of these issues:

1 Then what advantage has the Jew? Or what is the benefit of circumcision? **2** Great in every respect. First of all, that they were entrusted with the oracles of God.

The fact that Paul was the apostle to the Gentiles was very troublesome to many of the Jews. Gentiles were getting saved and the grace of God was evidenced in their lives. So, they complained, what good is it being a Jew? Look at all we have to do. If they can get saved without the Law of Moses or being circumcised, or being of the line of Abraham, then what is the purpose of being a Jew? It is all just a burden being the "chosen people of God."

So, Paul reminds them that they have the very words of God entrusted to them. What an amazing privilege. He is telling them to quit complaining and realize the treasure they have and be thankful for it. Paul is saying, "As a Jew, you have every advantage and blessing, but with that also comes responsibility."

> **3** What then? If some did not believe, their unbelief will not nullify the faithfulness of God, will it? **4** May it never be! Rather, let God be found true, though every man *be found* a liar, as it is written,
>
> "THAT YOU MAY BE JUSTIFIED IN YOUR WORDS,
> AND PREVAIL WHEN YOU ARE JUDGED."

Verses 1 and 2 basically challenged the sovereignty of God. The Jews had trouble understanding His sovereign choices. His ways are higher than the heavens, so that should not be too surprising. Now, in **verses 3 and 4**, they question God's faithfulness.

Since Israel had seen great trial and tribulation, they concluded that it must mean that God is not faithful to His promises. They are children of Abraham and heirs of His covenant promises and blessings. What happened to the blessings? Was the 70-year captivity a blessing from God? It must mean God is not faithful to His promises.

The Old Testament quote that Paul used in **Verse 4** comes from David's prayer in **Psalm 51.** David had been unfaithful with Bathsheba and asked God for mercy. Even when David was unfaithful to his nation, God still remained faithful to David. God demonstrated His faithfulness to David.. Nothing nullifies or cancels the faithfulness of God.

5 But if our unrighteousness demonstrates the righteous-ness of God, what shall we say? The God who inflicts wrath is not unrighteous, is He? (I am speaking in human terms.) **6** May it never be! For otherwise, how will God judge the world? **7** But if through my lie the truth of God abounded to His glory, why am I also still being judged as a sinner? **8** And why not *say* (as we are slanderously reported and as some claim that we say), "Let us do evil that good may come"? Their condemnation is just.

Finally, in this passage, the complaint is against the righteousness of God, and therefore, His authority and ability to rightfully judge us.

In **verse 5** Paul tells us he is using human reasoning to answer the complaints of God's people when he says "I am speaking in human terms." He is trying to say, "Just think about it and it makes sense."

Here is his logic - The very fact that sin and unrighteousness exists proves there must be a righteous standard to compare it to. God is that standard. He is fully righteous and all others do not meet His infinite perfection. Man, in comparison to God, is far below the perfection and righteousness of God. In conclusion, the existence of sin, or unrighteousness, proves the existence of true righteousness. It is like counterfeit money proves there is real money.

The second point in his logic is that if God is the perfect standard, always perfectly right, then He alone is the only one qualified to judge the world. He is the perfect Judge who will always judge rightly. That means, when God determines that sin must be punished and He inflicts wrath on the offender, then that wrath is a just judgment. He is always just in all His ways.

Paul then reminds the people that God, in His perfection, does not really need any help from us to be more righteous. When we sin, it only shows how righteous God is. We don't make God more righteous by sinning intentionally. It is foolish to think that way.

All the world is guilty before God (3:9-18)

9 What then? Are we better than they? Not at all; for we have already charged that both Jews and Greeks are all under sin;
10 as it is written,

"THERE IS NONE RIGHTEOUS, NOT EVEN ONE;
11 THERE IS NONE WHO UNDERSTANDS,
THERE IS NONE WHO SEEKS FOR GOD;
12 ALL HAVE TURNED ASIDE, TOGETHER THEY HAVE BE-COME USELESS;
THERE IS NONE WHO DOES GOOD,
THERE IS NOT EVEN ONE."
13 "THEIR THROAT IS AN OPEN GRAVE,
WITH THEIR TONGUES THEY KEEP DECEIVING,"
"THE POISON OF ASPS IS UNDER THEIR LIPS";
14 "WHOSE MOUTH IS FULL OF CURSING AND BITTERNESS";
15 "THEIR FEET ARE SWIFT TO SHED BLOOD,
16 DESTRUCTION AND MISERY ARE IN THEIR PATHS,
17 AND THE PATH OF PEACE THEY HAVE NOT KNOWN."
18 "THERE IS NO FEAR OF GOD BEFORE THEIR EYES."

This section brings up yet another view the Jews held. They thought they were better than the Gentile nations. They were upset with God and didn't understand His ways. They felt they were not sinners like the Gentiles.

9 "**What then? Are we better than they? Not at all; for we have already charged that both Jews and Greeks are all under sin;**"

Sin

The word "sin" is used hundreds of time in the Bible and has several uses:

- To be without a share in.
- To miss the mark.
- To err, be mistaken.
- To miss or wander from the path of uprightness and honor, to do or go wrong.
- To wander from the Law of God, violate God's Law, sin.
- A sin is any thought or action that falls short of God's perfect will or Law. God is perfect, and anything we do that falls short of His perfection is a sin.

One description in Scripture is that of an archer whose arrow misses the target. The target is the will of God, His holy, perfect plan. Another use of the word is that of a traveler who takes a wrong turn and does not get to the planned destination.

God has given us His perfect Word and has also placed a conscience in every person. We are without excuse in knowing right and wrong. Sin is also part of the fallen nature we have as children of Adam. The bottom line is that all have sinned, no exceptions, and we fall way short of God's glory. The problem is that other than having faith in Christ's finished work on the cross, there is no remedy for this ailment. It is a death sentence. However, Jesus paid it all and when we trust in that finished work, His death at Calvary satisfies our death sentence. As believers we are pardoned from the penalty we all deserve.

Paul begins quoting one Old Testament Scripture after another which describe the heart of every man as sinful. He is using their own Scriptures to prove they are just as sinful. It is always helpful to read the original Old Testament passages being quoted. At times, Paul, under the leading of the Holy Spirit, will combine several passages, or even leave out a phrase or two. It is all God's Word, and if God summarizes a longer passage or recombines several passages, that is completely up to Him. In **Chapter 9,** Paul quotes three separate sections from Hosea and combines them into one shorter statement that summarizes the message of Hosea. It shows how well Paul understood the message of the complete Word of God.

Let's do that. Let's read **Romans 3:10-19** and compare the entire Old Testament passage where the verses in Romans were taken.

"THERE IS NONE RIGHTEOUS, NOT EVEN ONE;
11 THERE IS NONE WHO UNDERSTANDS,
THERE IS NONE WHO SEEKS FOR GOD;
12 ALL HAVE TURNED ASIDE, TOGETHER THEY HAVE BECOME USELESS;
THERE IS NONE WHO DOES GOOD,
THERE IS NOT EVEN ONE."

Psalm 14:1-3

"The fool has said in his heart, "There is no God."
They are corrupt, they have committed abominable deeds;
There is no one who does good.
2 The Lord has looked down from heaven upon the sons of men
To see if there are any who understand, Who seek after God.
3 They have all turned aside, together they have become corrupt;
There is no one who does good, not even one."

Psalm 53:1-3

"The fool has said in his heart, "There is no God,"
They are corrupt, and have committed abominable injustice;
There is no one who does good.
2 God has looked down from heaven upon the sons of men
To see if there is anyone who understands, Who seeks after God.
3 Every one of them has turned aside; together they have become corrupt;
There is no one who does good, not even one."

13 "THEIR THROAT IS AN OPEN GRAVE,
WITH THEIR TONGUES THEY KEEP DECEIVING,"

"THE POISON OF ASPS IS UNDER THEIR LIPS";

Psalm 5:9

"There is nothing reliable in what they say;
Their inward part is destruction itself.
Their throat is an open grave;
They flatter with their tongue."

Psalm 140:3

"They have sharpened their tongues like a serpent; adders' poison [is] under their lips. Selah."

14 "WHOSE MOUTH IS FULL OF CURSING AND BITTERNESS";

Psalm 10:7

"His mouth is full of curses and deceit and oppression;
Under his tongue is mischief and wickedness."

15 "THEIR FEET ARE SWIFT TO SHED BLOOD,
16 DESTRUCTION AND MISERY ARE IN THEIR PATHS,
17 AND THE PATH OF PEACE THEY HAVE NOT KNOWN."

Proverbs 1:16

"For their feet run to evil
And they hasten to shed blood."

Isaiah 59:7,8

"Their feet run to evil,
And they hasten to shed innocent blood;
Their thoughts are thoughts of iniquity,
Devastation and destruction are in their highways.
[8] They do not know the way of peace,
And there is no justice in their tracks;
They have made their paths crooked,
Whoever treads on them does not know peace."

Psalm 36:1
"Transgression speaks to the ungodly within his heart;
There is no fear of God before his eyes."

Simple systematic theology on man's depravity

Not only did Paul recombine several Old Testament passages into a simplified summary of sin, but we also have something not commonly found in the Bible. Most doctrines, as we know them, are assembled from a wide source of Biblical verses. For example, if you wanted to study The Holy Spirit, you would not turn to one section of the Bible entitled "The Holy Spirit." You would have to search in many places and assemble what we know throughout the Bible to get a more complete picture. Since the Bible is not assembled according to themes, it is unusual to see an example of a developed theme.

Romans 3:9-18 is like a condensed systematic theology about the nature of man. If we have any questions about the depravity of man, these ten verses are a strong argument by themselves. There are, of course, many other passages in the Bible that deal with this subject. This short section of Romans taught the Roman church much about the nature of fallen man. Remember, the Jews did not think they were as bad as the Gentiles. Paul sets the record straight in **Chapter 3** that all men, Jew and Gentile, are desperately lost and need the salvation of God equally.

Summary - The depravity of man as revealed in Romans 3:9-18

• In man's natural state, no man is better off than another.

All men, Jew and Gentile are equally under the control of man's sinful nature **(9)**.

- No man is right before God naturally. We are all wrong. There is not a single exception. Sin has infected every human being. **(10)**.
- Unsaved man cannot understand spiritual things (**11**).
- Without God's intervention, no man on his own will seek God **(11).**
- Mankind, on its own, will always turn away from God **(12)**.
- We cannot do any truly, good thing for the Kingdom of God in our fallen state **(12)**.
- Our speech reflects our dead spirits. Everything we say condemns us. We poison others with our words **(13)**.
- We continually live in deception. We are deceived and we also deceive others around us. We are like snakes in the grass in our spirits, dangerous and poisonous **(13)**.
- We curse the One who made us, and we live with bitterness. Without the touch of God, we will never know joy or freedom from bitterness **(14)**.
- We are self-consumed to the point that, with very little thought, we can destroy others, even taking their lives. Everywhere we walk we bring misery to others **(15, 16)**. Our inclinations come, not from God, but from the Destroyer of our souls.
- Without God, we cannot experience peace in our lives. Our spirits are continually in a storm of unrest **(17)**.
- We know that the fear of God is the beginning of wisdom. However, the natural man does not have that healthy fear of God. Therefore, he is devoid of Godly wisdom and cannot make wise decisions **(18)**.

When we read **Romans 3:9-19**, we have a sense of what the depravity of man means. It does not mean that every man is as sinful as he can be. It means that every part of our being, our mind, our will, and emotions have been corrupted by sin. **Isaiah 64:6** provides a picture of this universal condition. *"We have all become like one who is unclean, and all our righteous deeds are like a polluted garment. We all fade like a leaf, and our iniquities, like the wind, take us away."*

Any Jew or Gentile reading this description in Romans of the natural man could not possibly think they were better than anyone else. Without God, we are a hopeless, deeply damaged, completely fallen humanity that needs God to rescue us. All of us.

GOOD NEWS IS COMING

The good news is just ahead. This chapter ends with the sun shining through the dark, miserable clouds of sin. There is a way that an unrighteous man can stand before God forgiven and cleansed. Man can be pardoned from the death row of sin and set free.

Paul's greatest desire was to preach the Gospel, the good news of Christ, to the Romans. First he needed to make sure that everyone understood the depth of the pollution of sin, and that we are incapable of fixing our problem. Only God could do that.

Justification by faith. Light in the darkness (3:19-31)

19 Now we know that whatever the Law says, it speaks to those who are under the Law, so that every mouth may be closed and all the world may become accountable to God; **20** because by the works of the Law no flesh will be justified in His sight; for through the Law *comes* the knowledge of sin. **21** But now apart from the Law *the* righteousness of God has been manifested, being witnessed by the

Law and the Prophets, **22** even *the* righteousness of God through faith in Jesus Christ for all those who believe; for there is no distinction; **23** for all have sinned and fall short of the glory of God, **24** being justified as a gift by His grace through the redemption which is in Christ Jesus; **25** whom God displayed publicly as a propitiation in His blood through faith. *This was* to demonstrate His righteousness, because in the forbearance of God He passed over the sins previously committed; **26** for the demonstration, *I say*, of His righteousness at the present time, so that He would be just and the justifier of the one who has faith in Jesus.

27 Where then is boasting? It is excluded. By what kind of law? Of works? No, but by a law of faith. **28** For we maintain that a man is justified by faith apart from works of the Law. **29** Or is God *the God* of Jews only? Is He not *the God* of Gentiles also? Yes, of Gentiles also, **30** since indeed God who will justify the circumcised by faith and the uncircumcised through faith is one.

31 Do we then nullify the Law through faith? May it never be! On the contrary, we establish the Law.

Light is now about to flood into the dark room. This last section of **Romans 3** is packed with hope for all men trapped in sin. It is a beautiful and logical progression. First, Paul gives a clear and irrefutable proof that all men are sinners and have no way to solve their problem. Then, he presents the solution to the problem that comes from God, the only One who could have done it.

The major themes in this section have filled hundreds upon hundreds of commentaries and have supplied the information and materials for thousands of sermons and lessons.

For a moment just let your mind think about these major themes from Romans **3:19-31**.

- The purpose of the Law of God
- Man's accountability to God
- Justification by faith
- The righteousness of God
- Faith
- The finished work of Jesus Christ
- The universal fallenness of mankind
- The glory of God
- Salvation, the gift
- The grace of God
- Redemption
- Propitiation, or the satisfaction, of God's righteous requirements
- The adequacy of the blood of Christ
- God's forbearance, patience with sinful man
- Jews and Gentiles alike can be saved

Numerous books have been written on each of these points. One of Paul's styles was to pack a lot of teachings into a small space. Example - **Ephesians 1:3-14**, in one continuous sentence, Paul includes 35 major doctrines. He only has 15 in **Romans 3:19-31**!

D. Martyn Lloyd-Jones, the famous preacher in England, spent many of his preaching years in Romans. After his death, his messages filled 14 volumes. After reading the doctrines just in this passage of **Romans 3**, you can see why a teacher or preacher could find a lifetime of messages and lessons just from these few verses. It is basically the entire message of the Bible.

Here is a short summary of Romans 3:19-31 written by taking the 15 doctrines in the order they are listed:

God gave His Law to His fallen world so that every man would be convicted and convinced of his sin. Each man must stand before God and is responsible for his own sinful behavior. Every man is condemned because of his sin and is unable to fix the broken relationship between himself and his Creator. However, God, who is righteous, has made a way for an unrighteous man to be brought into a right relationship with Himself. He has offered a pardon (a legal proclamation) freeing guilty mankind from facing the eternal death penalty that he deserves.

He has provided this undeserved pardon (justification) to all men. We receive it by faith, based on the finished work of God's Son, Jesus Christ. God is satisfied with the work of Jesus. This gift of salvation is offered to all men. We who have been enslaved by sin all our lives are offered freedom. We have been purchased back from the slave market of sin (redeemed) and released from sin's bondage, because the death of Jesus has satisfied the wrath of God against sin. The death of Christ in our place was enough to secure eternal life for all who believe, both Jew and Gentile.

Amen.

Romans 4

FOR WHAT DOES THE SCRIPTURE SAY? "ABRAHAM BELIEVED GOD, AND IT WAS CREDITED TO HIM AS RIGHTEOUSNESS."

CHAPTER OVERVIEW

- **We are all sinners.** We can't make ourselves right with God, so we have nothing to boast about.

- **God solved the problem** and can now credit us with the righteousness of Christ. It is not something we have worked for and earned. Christ did the work. By grace, we receive the benefits of His work.

- **The Jews depended on their own efforts**, religious practices, and circumcision to obtain God's acceptance. It isn't like a job where someone gets paid for their work. No amount of personal effort will get anyone to Heaven.

- **Abraham had faith in God,** and he was declared righteous by God because of that faith. He wasn't justified by his works, being circumcised, or keeping the Law. Now, all who believe, like Abraham, can be declared in right standing before God, both Jew and Gentile.

Key verses for Chapter 4

² For if Abraham was justified by works, he has something to boast about, but not before God. ³ For what does the Scripture say? "ABRAHAM BELIEVED GOD, AND IT WAS CREDITED TO HIM AS RIGHTEOUSNESS."

SIMPLE OUTLINE

I. How is a man Justified? (4:1-15)

    A. Man is not justified by works. (4:1-7)

    B. Man is not justified by religion. (4:8-12)

    C. Man is not justified through the Law. (4:13-15)

II. Justification is available to all who believe. (4:16-25)

    A. Justification is by grace through faith. (4:16-17)

    B. Abraham, an example of faith. (4:18-22)

    C. Christ was raised for our justification. (4:23-25)

Romans 4 Commentary

How is a man justified? (4:1-15)
Man is not justified by works (4:1-7)

1 What then shall we say that Abraham, our forefather according to the flesh, has found? **2** For if Abraham was justified by works, he has something to boast about, but not before God. **3** For what does the Scripture say? "Abraham believed God, and it was credited to him as righteousness." **4** Now to the one who works, his wage is not credited as a favor, but as what is due. **5** But to the one who does not work, but believes in Him who justifies the ungodly, his faith is credited as righteousness, **6** just as David also speaks of the blessing on the man to whom God credits righteousness apart from works:

7 "Blessed are those whose lawless deeds have been forgiven, and whose sins have been covered.

Sin is universal, all have sinned. Most religions in the world recognize they fall short of perfection. Some call it sin and others describe it differently. Everyone knows we miss the mark. Nobody is perfect. The following is how some of the major world religions deal with sin:

Islam. (Quran 7:6–9). A Muslim can become righteous through prayer, alms-giving, fasting, and living according to the Quran. It is by human effort, or good works, a Muslim hopes to be purified from his sin. A person becomes his own savior if he does everything right.

Hinduism. There is no actual, single, holy God, so there is not really any accountability for sin. People do evil things, but Karma, the law of cosmic sowing and reaping, will eventually balance all things in the universe. We each will go through a series of births and rebirths and ultimately be purged of evil. They become one with everything, whatever that means! So, in essence, sin is not a problem. It will all work out on its own.

Buddhism. Like Hinduism, Buddhists see life as a cycle of births and rebirths. Buddhists do not believe in God, or any gods. Man is just part of nature. All problems are caused by man's desires, so they use meditation and prayer to cleanse their minds and end the struggle with desire until they reach nirvana, the day when all desire is conquered. Then, they are free from the cycle of life and death. Buddhists do not believe in sin.

Christianity. There is one God Almighty, Maker of heaven and earth. Mankind sinned and now all are born in sin. We can't solve our own sin problem, so God did. He sent His beloved Son, who died and rose again to pay for our sins and give us eternal life as a gift. It is by the grace of God that we are made clean and declared righteous before God, based solely on the work of Christ on the cross. It is in Christ alone that we find forgiveness for our sins.

> **7 "Blessed are those whose lawless deeds have been forgiven, and whose sins have been covered."**

As Christians, we understand that sin is real. We have a relationship with God. We have forgiveness of sin and peace with our Creator. Unlike any other religion, we have real hope. It is not based on what we do or have done, but on God Himself and what He has done. The difference between all world religions and Christianity comes down to two words. The world tries to "do," but Christ has said, "Done!"

Verses 1 and 2 are clear that Abraham, the forefather of the Jewish religion, was not made right in the sight of God by any human effort. He had nothing in himself to brag or boast about. It was all of God.

Verses 3-5 compares the difference between being justified by faith and the one who tries to be justified by his own works. A person who has a job gets paid for his work. Some felt becoming righteous was the same. They thought if a person did good works, he got paid by earning righteousness. But it doesn't work that way. We just read in **Romans 3** that our righteousness is filthy rags. But what we could not do, God did in sending His Son to pay for our sin. When we accept that, His righteousness is credited to our bankrupt spiritual accounts.

Verses 6 and 7 add the example of David. David, while king, sinned greatly. He committed adultery and murder. He repented and was forgiven by God, but it cost him dearly in the death of his son born through Bathsheba. David, as a fallen sinner, could not solve his sin problem. The death of his son was the result of his sin. That sin also caused the death of God's Son. Our sin has done the same. David's sin was forgiven by turning to God and seeking forgiveness. It was by faith that David, like Abraham, found peace with God. Righteousness came by faith for both of them. **Verse 7** is praise from **Psalm 32:7** after David was pardoned by God for his sins. His forgiveness, pardon, and justification, came by faith in God.

Man is not justified by his works.

MAN IS NOT JUSTIFIED BY RELIGION (4:8-12)

8 "Blessed is the man whose sin the Lord will not take into account."

9 Is this blessing then on the circumcised, or on the uncircumcised also? For we say, "Faith was credited to Abraham as righteousness." **10** How then was it credited? While he was circumcised, or uncircumcised? Not while circumcised, but while uncircumcised; **11** and he received the sign of circumcision, a seal of the righteousness of the faith which he had while uncircumcised, so that he might be the father of all who believe without being circumcised, that righteousness might be credited to them, **12** and the father of circumcision to those who not only are of the circumcision, but who also follow in the steps of the faith of our father Abraham which he had while uncircumcised.

Verse 8 begins by showing us the distinctive concept of justification. It does not mean we are made innocent. This text tells us that a man's sin is no longer considered against him. It is no longer taken into account. The sin does not cease to exist, it just has no claim against the sinner. Our sin is no longer held against us. It was held against Christ, and the penalty the sin earned was paid in full by Jesus on Calvary.

Verses 9 and 10 are a clarification of the relationship between circumcision and faith. Abraham is the example. Abraham believed God and demonstrated this faith by following all that God told him. It was the faith of Abraham that God honored. Because of that faith, God made a covenant with him. Abraham became the father of the children of Israel. The sign of the Abrahamic covenant was the act of circumcision. It came after Abraham was justified by his faith, not before it. Circumcision is not what makes a person a true child of Abraham, but faith is what justifies.

Baptism is a parallel concept. Baptism does not make a person a Christian, it is a public sign of a person's salvation which is by faith and faith alone. Circumcision was the sign of the covenant God made with Abraham and his children. It came after faith, not before it.

Verses 11 and 12 present the hope that faith is for all, both Jew and Gentile. **Verse 11** explains that Abraham was made right with God by faith. Circumcision had nothing to do with his acceptance by God. Gentiles who don't have the covenant sign of circumcision, can also be made right with God through faith. **Verse 11** tells us that Abraham is the father of all the uncircumcised who have faith in God. **Verse 12** reminds the Jews that Abraham is the father of all of Israel who have faith, the faith that Abraham had before he was circumcised. These verses are clear that neither circumcision nor non-circumcision, are what is important. The only thing necessary for a man to be right with God is to have faith in Him.

Man is not justified by religion.

MAN IS NOT JUSTIFIED THROUGH THE LAW (4:13-15)

13 For the promise to Abraham or to his descendants that he would be heir of the world was not through the Law but through the righteousness of faith. **14** For if those who are of the Law are heirs, faith is made void and the promise is nullified; **15** for the Law brings about wrath, but where there is no law, there also is no violation.

No human effort or ceremony of circumcision can make a man right with God. **Verses 13-15** teach that following the Law of God is also on the list of things that can't make a man right with

God. We have previously seen that the purpose of the Law was to show man how sinful he was. No man can meet the demands of the moral law of God. We all fall short. The Law is like a mirror which exposes our sin. **Verse 15** adds to this by explaining that those who claim they are under the Law are condemned by that Law. Therefore they are under the wrath of God. If all we have to cling to is the Law, then we are condemned by that Law and will face the wrath of our Holy God. **Verse 14** explains why. When we claim the Law as our path to salvation, we don't follow the true path of faith, but a false path of self-righteousness.

Once again, we find a path that does not lead to life but ends up facing the wrath of God. **Verse 13** begins this third section with the clear statement that Abraham was not made right with God by keeping the Law of God. The Law, given to Moses, came hundreds of years after Abraham. So, Abraham was credited with righteousness by faith. He believed and obeyed God.

Man is not justified by keeping the Law.

SUMMARY OF THE FIRST SECTION OF ROMANS 4:1-15

Abraham was not made right with God by any human effort, but by faith in God. Abraham was not made right with God by circumcision but by faith in God. Abraham was not made righteous before God by keeping the moral Law of God. It was faith, faith, faith.

Romans 4:16-25 will show how Abraham demonstrated his faith. First we need to be clear about Justification

What is Justification?

JUSTIFICATION

Justification is a major theme in the Epistle to the Romans. Justification is the declaring of a person to be just, or righteous. It does not mean a person is innocent. It is a legal term signifying the acquittal of a crime. It is a legal pardon. It means we are no longer held accountable for our crime. God remains just and the justifier of the ungodly. His justice has been satisfied in Christ's substitutionary death on the cross. God poured out His just wrath on His Son, who paid the complete penalty for our sin. That was possible because He was fully man and also fully God. Now that the punishment is over, God can credit our spiritual accounts with the righteousness of His Son. We, as guilty sinners who have been pardoned, now stand before God as righteous, just as if we had never sinned. Our role in all this is to simply trust the work of Christ and accept His justification as a gift.

Justification is available to all who believe (4:16-25)

16 For this reason *it is* by faith, in order that *it may be* in accordance with grace, so that the promise will be guaranteed to all the descendants, not only to those who are of the Law, but also to those who are of the faith of Abraham, who is the father of us all, **17** (as it is written, "A FATHER OF MANY NATIONS HAVE I MADE YOU") IN THE PRESENCE OF HIM WHOM HE BELIEVED, *even* God, who gives life to the dead and calls into being that which does not exist.

> **"Grace and faith work in harmony, like a team of horses pulling the same chariot, but grace and human works are contrary the one to the other and pull opposite ways, and therefore God has not chosen to yoke them together. Nor will he make an image partly of gold and partly of clay"**
> (Charles Spurgeon)

When we come to God through faith, grace takes over. Salvation is either a work of man or of God. Any work we do to earn salvation is saying to God, "Jesus' death on the cross was not enough, not quite finished." When you think of the thief on the cross who simply said, "Lord, remember me," everything changed forever even after a lifetime of sin and guilt. An old hymn said it well, "Nothing in my hand I bring, simply to the cross I cling." When Jesus became our sin on the cross **(2 Corinthians 5:21)** and bore all the Holy wrath of the Father for our sins and then said it was finished, it was finished. All of it. Now, the Father is free to pardon each of us when He looks through the blood of His Son. He sees a child of God, made righteous, justified by the death and resurrection of Christ. What can any man possibly add to that?

Who does this apply to? **Verse 16** says it is for all who are of the Law and for those who are of the faith of Abraham. Who are these two? In the Epistle, Paul addresses the complete Church made up of both Jew and Gentile believers. He addresses the

81

individual backgrounds and issues each face and works to unify the Church into one body in Christ.

The phrase **"of the Law"** refers to Jews who have believed in the Messiah. They are the people of the Law of Moses who have found peace with God through faith. They formerly relied on following the Law of God, however, all that did was expose their sins and their inability to keep it. The Law drove them to Christ, to faith where they found life. That was ultimately the end purpose of the Law in the first place.

The phrase **"of the faith of Abraham"** refers to the believing Gentiles. Those who were outside the covenants of God by birth but have believed in Christ as Messiah, are now grafted into the family tree of God's complete family. The Jews learned that religion cannot save but always ends with the wrath of God. The Gentiles learned no good deed can overcome the fallen nature of man. Both groups came the same way, by faith, as Abraham came by faith. Now, both groups of believers, those Jews who were "by the law" and Gentiles who simply came by the same "faith of Abraham," have both become one family, children of Abraham. They both now can refer to Abraham as their father.

> [26] **"For you are all sons of God through faith in Christ Jesus.** [27] **For all of you who were baptized into Christ have clothed yourselves with Christ.** [28] **There is neither Jew nor Greek, there is neither slave nor free man, there is neither male nor female; for you are all one in Christ Jesus.** [29] **And if you belong to Christ, then you are Abraham's descendants, heirs according to promise."**
> (Galatians 3:26-29)

Verse 17 shows that the bringing together of Jew and Gentile into one family was prophesied to Abraham. It was a work of God, of grace, **"God, who gives life to the dead and calls into**

being that which does not exist." In **Ephesians Chapter 2 and 3**, Paul refers to this as a great mystery, hidden from time past, but now revealed in the New Testament time.

> [4] **"By referring to this, when you read you can understand my insight into the mystery of Christ,** [5] **which in other generations was not made known to the sons of men, as it has now been revealed to His holy apostles and prophets in the Spirit;** [6] **to be specific, that the Gentiles are fellow heirs and fellow members of the body, and fellow partakers of the promise in Christ Jesus through the gospel . . . "**
>
> (Ephesians 3:4-6)

The next several verses describe in more detail the faith of Abraham.

ABRAHAM, AN EXAMPLE OF FAITH (4:18-22)

18 In hope against hope he believed, so that he might become a father of many nations according to that which had been spoken, "SO SHALL YOUR DESCENDANTS BE." **19** Without becoming weak in faith he contemplated his own body, now as good as dead since he was about a hundred years old, and the deadness of Sarah's womb; **20** yet, with respect to the promise of God, he did not waver in unbelief but grew strong in faith, giving glory to God, **21** and being fully assured that what God had promised, He was able also to perform. **22** Therefore IT WAS ALSO CREDITED TO HIM AS RIGHTEOUSNESS.

Verse 18, "Hope against hope." The phrase can sound a bit confusing, but it is actually quite simple. It is saying that Abraham found his hope in God when hope in himself and his circumstances seemed impossible. Abraham was very aged, as was Sarah, when God told them they would have a family. The world would be blessed by his family line. Both Abraham and Sarah were barren and beyond the natural age to have children. The promise of God had no hope in them, in their natural bodies. It seemed hopeless.

Abraham believed God, in spite of the hopeless condition of his and Sarah's flesh. Abraham had hope when there seemed to be no hope. "In hope against hope he believed." He had hope when there was no hope. He had God.

> **"There is no pit so deep that God is not deeper."**
> (Corrie Ten Boom)

Verses 19-21 expand on the seemingly hopeless condition of their aged bodies, and yet, the faith of Abraham still grew stronger. He chose to believe God over his outward circumstances. Abraham was 100 years old; Sarah was not far behind him. Instead of questioning God and why He waited so long, Abraham believed God. The result of that belief is found in **verse 22.**

Verse 22 is a quote from **Genesis 15**.

> [5] **"And He took him outside and said, "Now look toward the heavens, and count the stars, if you are able to count them." And He said to him, "So shall your descendants be."** [6] **Then he believed in the Lord; and He reckoned it to him as righteousness."** (Genesis 15:5,6)

Because Abraham believed "what God had promised, He was able also to perform," God "credited" it to him as righteousness. This is an important concept to understand. Greek lexicons tell us this means to "impute something to someone." The English dictionary adds that to impute means "to associate (righteousness, guilt, etc.), to someone by virtue of a similar quality in another."

In easy English, it means Abraham was given a new standing with God because of his faith.

HOW CAN A JUST GOD JUSTIFY AN UNJUST MAN?

How can God do this? How can God, who is Holy, declare that a sinner is no longer accountable for the sin and crimes committed? We know sin brings the wrath of God. We have seen that since **Chapter 1**. Can God just ignore the offense of sin against His Holy nature?

The answer was found in the previous chapter, **Romans 3:26**:

> **"He did it to demonstrate his righteousness at the present time, so as to be just and the one who justifies those who have faith in Jesus."** (Romans 3:26)

The word that makes all the difference is "Jesus." God must judge sin, He cannot ignore justice. God poured out His Holy wrath on His Son, instead of on us. In doing so, the requirements of punishment for sin were met when Christ became our sin on the cross and bore the deserved punishment for us. Now, we stand forgiven and credited with God's righteousness. We are pardoned, justified, free to be children of God. That is grace.

> **"He made Him who knew no sin to be sin on our behalf, so that we might become the righteousness of God in Him."**
> (2 Corinthians 5:21)

Christ was raised for our justification (4:23-25)

23 Now not for his sake only was it written that it was credited to him, **24** but for our sake also, to whom it will be credited, as those who believe in Him who raised Jesus our Lord from the dead, **25** *He* who was delivered over because of our transgressions, and was raised because of our justification.

One way to understand this is to picture a vile murderer sitting on death row, rightfully condemned to pay the ultimate penalty for his crime. He had taken a life, now he must forfeit his own. As he sits on death row awaiting his final doom, he knows he is guilty and deserves his punishment. He is a dead man, staring at the gallows, awaiting the actual moment that will end his sinful life.

The unthinkable happens. The sovereign of the land, the king himself, has mercy on the man and sends a letter of pardon and reprieve. The execution is canceled. Why? Did the sinner deserve it, or do something to earn this favor? No, it was totally a sovereign decision by the king who has the legal authority to pardon a man.

The Bible shows us we are all on death row (see the first three chapters of Romans). We deserve death. Nothing we can do will atone for our sin. Nothing! There is One who can atone and that is what He did. An innocent man, who is also God, went to the gallows for us and died our death, a life for a life. The penalty was paid in our place. The penalty is covered and justice has been served. Jesus died, we are freed from the penalty of our sin. We can now be legally pardoned by the King. It is possible because the law was carried out. Life was given for a life. That is why the King, the Sovereign, can remain Just, and still the Justifier of the ungodly.

As proof that death has been turned to life, Jesus rose from the dead, and now guarantees that we, formerly death-condemned criminals, will also rise. Jesus' proof of life is our proof of eternal life.

We are risen with Him (**Ephesians 1 and 2**). He was raised for our justification.

Amen and amen!

Is Paul finished with the topic of Justification?

The answer is Chapter 5. There is a lot more to say.

Romans 5
The Impact of Adam's Sin

. . . "through one man sin entered
into the world, and death through
sin, and so death spread to all
men, because all sinned" . . .

(Romans 5:10)

CHAPTER OVERVIEW

Chapters 4 and 5 go together. They are a strong, logical presentation of the crown jewel of salvation, justification. **Chapter 4** teaches us that a person cannot be made right with God by any human work, any religious practice, or by following the Law of God. Faith is the only key that unlocks the door to a relationship with God. Once that door is opened, the blessings of God are available and numerous. **Chapter 5** is a look at the jewel itself in all its glory. Like a stunning faceted diamond, each side reflecting light, **Chapter 5** displays the various blessings and benefits of justification. This jewel was purchased at a great price, God's own Son.

Key verses for Chapter 5

[17] **"For if by the transgression of the one, death reigned through the one, much more those who receive the abundance of grace and of the gift of righteousness will reign in life through the One, Jesus Christ."**

SIMPLE OUTLINE

I. Romans 5:1-11. The blessings of justification. God has justified believers and has showered them with numerous blessings. Justification leads to sanctification and on to glorification.

II. Romans 5:12-14. The impact of Adam's sin. The sin of Adam plunged the human race into sin and brought death on all mankind.

III. Romans 5:15-21. The reason for Christ's sacrifice. The sacrifice of Christ, the second Adam, provides salvation and eternal life to anyone who believes the Gospel.

Romans 5 Commentary

Romans 5:1-11.
The blessings of justification.

1 Therefore, having been justified by faith, we have peace with God through our Lord Jesus Christ, **2** through whom also we have obtained our introduction by faith into this grace in which we stand; and we exult in hope of the glory of God. **3** And not only this, but we also exult in our tribulations, knowing that tribulation brings about perseverance; **4** and perseverance, proven character; and proven character, hope; **5** and hope does not disappoint, because the love of God has been poured out within our hearts through the Holy Spirit who was given to us.

6 For while we were still helpless, at the right time Christ died for the ungodly. **7** For one will hardly die for a righteous man; though perhaps for the good man someone would dare even to die. **8** But God demonstrates His own love toward us, in that while we were yet sinners, Christ died for us. **9** Much more then, having now been justified by His blood, we shall be saved from the wrath *of God* through Him. **10** For if while we were enemies we were reconciled to God through the death of His Son, much more, having been reconciled, we shall be saved by His life. **11** And not only this, but we also exult in God through our Lord Jesus Christ, through whom we have now received the reconciliation.

Grace

Rather than give a technical definition, I prefer to tell a story.

A young street boy, living in poverty, grows up without parents to guide him. He steals some food from a local food vendor at an outdoor market. He is caught by the owner. The owner shows **mercy** by not turning him over to the police. He didn't get what he deserved, he was spared imprisonment. The owner goes further. He provides a wonderful meal for the child and gives him money for some future meals. That would be **compassion, a loving act**. The man arranges to adopt the child into his own family and give him his family name and makes him an heir to everything he has. Grace is getting what he did not deserve. The same grace is what we have received.

We have been spared from the wrath of God, shown mercy, and adopted into His family. We are given the family name and inheritance. We have been blessed beyond anything we could ever deserve or even dream about. We have become recipients of **God's grace**. Justification is a gift of God's grace.

Here is a list, like a miniature Bible Dictionary, of the blessings we experience when we are made right with God when we are justified by faith in Christ. Each of these blessings is listed in the order they appear in **Chapter 5:1-11**.

- Justification by faith. We have received a legal pardon from having to pay the just penalty for our sin. We no longer face the wrath of God.
- We have peace with God.
- We receive grace from God.
- We have a future hope of the Glory of God.
- We rejoice that testing and suffering result in our becoming more like Christ.
- Sanctification. Godliness being built in our lives now empowers us each day to be more like Christ.
- We receive a hope that never disappoints.
- The love of God is poured out in our hearts.
- The Holy Spirit indwells each of us.
- When we were most helpless and still in our sin, God rescued us. We are always on His mind and in His heart.
- Reconciliation. Formerly enemies of God, separated by sin, we are now friends with God.

Salvation is commonly thought of as having our sins forgiven. We are given eternal life. As true as that is, it falls very short of describing all that happens to a believer. In **Chapter 1:18-32** we read about a landslide of sin. **Chapter 5** describes another landslide, this time it comes from God. This is a landslide of grace. When a person comes into a living relationship with God many things happen. It is the beginning of a totally new life.

The old life was one of slavery to sin, condemned by God and under His eternal wrath. We had no hope in the future or power to live free of sin in this life. We were at odds with God. Our spirits are in constant turmoil and without peace in our daily struggle.

Chapter 5 tells the new story. Being legally pardoned, justified by God, we finally have peace in our lives. We have been reconciled to God. The power of sin's control has been broken. God, not sin, is our new Master, The Holy Spirit dwells within us, God's love, grace, and peace flood into our hearts. The righteousness of Christ is entered into God's ledger book. The power to live lives pleasing to our God becomes available to us. Yes, it is a much larger picture than only having our sins forgiven and on our way to Heaven.

VERSES 7, 8
WHO IS THE RIGHTEOUS MAN AND WHO IS THE GOOD MAN?

> **7** "For one will hardly die for a righteous man; though perhaps for the good man someone would dare even to die. **8** But God demonstrates His own love toward us, in that while we were yet sinners, Christ died for us."

Verses 7 and 8 give an important contrast between a man's heart and the heart of God. The righteous man, or self-righteous man, represents the Pharisees and others who seek to attain righteousness by self-effort. The good man is more genuine, having a good heart and helping his fellow man for the right reasons. The point of these two verses is that most people would find it hard, if not impossible, to give their lives to save a Pharisee or self-righteous type of person. A few would give their lives to rescue a good man, even then, few might give their lives for the best part of humanity. Christ gave His life for the worst, the very ones who mocked and killed Him. The love and grace of God are without comparison.

Romans 5 is a good chapter to read often to remind ourselves of the many blessings we have in Christ. The believers in Rome were undergoing intense persecution, and many were killed for their faith. These words of Paul would have been very encouraging. His words found in **verse 3** assured them that even the greatest trial they faced was used by God to make them more like Christ. They were assured that they would never lose the love, the grace, the hope, the peace and their relationship with God no matter what happened. They had a present hope and future hope.

And so do we!

Romans 5:12-14
The Impact of Adam's sin.

12 Therefore, just as through one man sin entered into the world, and death through sin, and so death spread to all men, because all sinned— **13** for until the Law sin was in the world, but sin is not imputed when there is no law. **14** Nevertheless death reigned from Adam until Moses, even over those who had not sinned in the likeness of the offense of Adam, who is a type of Him who was to come.

In these three verses, Paul takes us back to when sin entered the human race. It is important to understand that the name "Adam" in Hebrew means "mankind." "Adam", when used in **Genesis 5**, refers to both Adam and Eve as mankind or the human race. At that point in time, they were the only two people on the earth, the human race.

> **¹This is the book of the generations of Adam. In the day that God created man, in the likeness of God made he him;** **² Male and female created he them; and blessed them, and called their name Adam, in the day when they were created.** (Genesis 5:1.2)

When Adam and Eve chose to disobey God, the entire human

race fell. Each person on the earth today is a descendant of that fallen couple. We are all born in the likeness of Adam - fallen. Since God had warned that death would be the result of disobeying Him, the human race entered into death when the human race sinned. And we are all born of Adam and death spread to all of us because we are the seed of Adam, Adam's fallen family. That is the background of **Romans 5:12.**

Verses 13 and 14 describe what happened next. Death reigned over the entire human race. Even people that had not shown the same kind of disobedience to God, as Adam had, also died. Sin, like a plague, affects everyone. It is a serious spiritual birth defect that exempts no one. Even those who lived before the Law that was given to Moses died.

Verse 13 is difficult to understand and theologians debate it. Was man held accountable for his sin before the Law of Moses?

Sodom and Gomorrah are examples of a people who lived in a depraved condition before the Law of Moses had been given. Lot, Abraham's nephew, lived in their midst. Lot, although compromised, was a righteous man. God later sent Angels as a warning to the people of their sin and approaching judgment. The people were told their acts were evil. We know how that story ended — death and judgment. Man is accountable to the Creator. There is a moral law built into each man (**Romans 1 and 2**). Even if those before the Law were not held accountable for Adam's specific sin, they, like we, were still sinners by birth, accountable for violating the moral law and conscience built into every man. Even remote tribes today internally know killing someone or stealing their property is wrong.

Since the fall of Adam, sin reigned over the entire human race. Noah's flood is another good example. Noah was called righteous, and the world at that time was called evil. They did not have the Law of Moses, but they and Noah knew that evil and sin were active. Noah preached for over 100 years to that rebellious and sinful generation. Eventually, God sent the flood as a judgment against sin.

Romans 5:15-21
The reason for Christ's sacrifice.

15 But the free gift is not like the transgression. For if by the transgression of the one the many died, much more did the grace of God and the gift by the grace of the one Man, Jesus Christ, abound to the many. **16** The gift is not like *that which came* through the one who sinned; for on the one hand the judgment *arose* from one *transgression* resulting in condemnation, but on the other hand the free gift *arose* from many transgressions resulting in justification. **17** For if by the transgression of the one, death reigned through the one, much more those who receive the abundance of grace and of the gift of righteousness will reign in life through the One, Jesus Christ.

18 So then as through one transgression there resulted condemnation to all men, even so through one act of righteousness there resulted justification of life to all men. **19** For as through the one man's disobedience the many were made sinners, even so through the obedience of the One the many will be made righteous. **20** The Law came in so that the transgression would increase; but where sin increased, grace abounded all the more, **21** so that, as sin reigned in death, even so grace would reign through righteousness to eternal life through Jesus Christ our Lord.

Verse 15 — Adam sinned — all died. Christ died so all could live. Adam's sin brought a curse. Christ's sacrifice provides grace.

Verse 16 — Adam's single sin brought judgment on the world. Christ's gift of justification came as a response to the transgressions of the many. Where sin abounded, grace did much more abound.

Verse 17, 18 — The sin of Adam established the reign of sin for the human race. The gift of Christ has a much greater impact on the human race. He has erased the final consequences of death and has substituted His righteousness for our unrighteousness. He has removed our condemnation and given us eternal life.

Verse 19 — The disobedience of one man, Adam, made all men sinners. The obedience of the One man, Christ, made many righteous.

Verse 20 — The Law was given to bring awareness of sin. The exposure to the knowledge of sin revealed the depth of sin in the human heart and guilt increased. It is that knowledge of the depth of sin that will drive a person to God to find forgiveness and grace. So as man's sin increased, grace abounded even more. Knowledge of sin is the first step in repentance and finding eternal life.

A good example is the rich young ruler. The man thought he was good. Jesus explained what the Law really meant, and for the first time the young man realized that he was a sinner and a great sinner at that. That was the only way that the self-righteous young man had any hope of finding eternal life. How that story ends is not recorded. By exposing the man's need by using the Law, the man, for the first time, understood he was a sinner. Grace was at the doorstep and all he needed to do was step in.

Verse 21- Paul concludes that sin and death have reigned from the beginning, resulting in mankind being cut off from God forever. In contrast, grace will reign forever. Believers have been made righteousness and brought into family relationship with God through Jesus Christ.

Summary of Chapters 4 and 5

In all the world, in all of human history, no greater thought can be found than the guilty are set free, no longer having to pay for their crimes. An innocent One stepped up and paid for our crimes and that payment was enough to set us free, forever. And not just us but for everyone in the world who believes. Where is there a greater story or hope?

> **"He that spared not his own Son, but delivered him up for us all, how shall he not with him also freely give us all things?"** (Romans 8:32)

COMING UP

Since we have been set free from the bondage of sin and death, how shall we believers understand and deal with sin today? Does that mean we never sin again? What is our relationship to the Law now that we have been declared righteous? As Christians, why do we still struggle with sin and the flesh if it has been defeated?

These and other questions will be dealt with in **Chapters 6 and 7**

General Introduction to Romans Chapters 6-8

SIN AND THE BELIEVER

Romans Chapters 1-5 began with our fallen human race. God is Righteous and we are unrighteous. Everyone has sinned, no exceptions. We learned that faith changes everything. When we trusted Christ we became part of the family of God. We have been legally pardoned by God, also called justified. The journey took us from being identified with the fallen world to becoming part of God's forever family.

This next section, **Romans chapters 6-8**, will explain the relationship, we as believers, now have with sin. We have been freed from sin's mastery. We still are not free from its presence and influence. God has provided the resources for us to live victoriously in spite of the inner battle we struggle with daily. In the end, we are held tightly in the hands of our loving and powerful God. We are in his family forever.

CHAINS OF SIN BROKEN,
FREE AT LAST
AND ALIVE TO GOD

CHAPTER OVERVIEW

We have been made right with God. We, who were formerly un-righteous, are now children of God. The righteousness of Christ has been entered into our spiritual accounts. That is called Justification and was explained in **Chapters 4 and 5.** In **Chapter 6,** we now see, as believers, we are considered dead to sin. The slavery to sin we knew before we came to Christ is now broken. We are free from that slavery. We, who were spiritually dead, are now very much alive to God because of Christ. We have been delivered from the evil slave-owner of sin. We are now willing slaves of Christ. We have changed masters. As slaves of righteousness, we have exchanged a life leading to death for one that leads to eternal life.

Key verses - Chapter 6:13, 14

[13] and do not go on presenting the members of your body to sin as instruments of unrighteousness; but present yourselves to God as those alive from the dead, and your members as instruments of righteousness to God. [14] For sin shall not be master over you, for you are not under law but under grace.

SIMPLE OUTLINE

I. Romans 6:1-7. We are dead to sin.

II. Romans 6:8-11. Alive to God in Christ.

III. Romans 6:12-14. Rejecting sin as your master.

IV. Romans 6:15-19. Changing masters.

V. Romans 6:20-23. From a life leading to death to one leading to life.

Romans 6:1-7
We are dead to sin.

1 What shall we say then? Are we to continue in sin so that grace may increase? **2** May it never be! How shall we who died to sin still live in it? **3** Or do you not know that all of us who have been baptized into Christ Jesus have been baptized into His death? **4** Therefore we have been buried with Him through baptism into death, so that as Christ was raised from the dead through the glory of the Father, so we too might walk in newness of life. **5** For if we have become united with *Him* in the likeness of His death, certainly we shall also be *in the likeness* of His resurrection, **6** knowing this, that our old self was crucified with *Him*, in order that our body of sin might be done away with, so that we would no longer be slaves to sin; **7** for he who has died is freed from sin.

SIN AND GRACE (6:1,2)

1 What shall we say then? Are we to continue in sin so that grace may increase? **2** May it never be! How shall we who died to sin still live in it?

Where sin abounds, grace abounds more. Some believers thought that sin was good because it produced more grace. It was used as an excuse to sin. Paul says this is bad thinking. Sin never has a good purpose. We are not to tempt God. God does not need our help with His grace. We have been crucified with Christ **(Galatians 2:20).** Sin does not need to continue to be our master. Jesus is our Master. We honor Him when we avoid sin, not by participating in it. Sin no longer has the legal right to control our lives.

Baptism

Baptism is not what saves a person. It is, however, an important step of obedience for a believer. When we commit our lives to Jesus Christ, we are transformed by the Lord, our old life has passed away, a new life has begun. The way we testify to the world that a spiritual change has happened is by water baptism. It is the outward symbol of the inward change that God makes in our lives. Baptism symbolizes we are buried with Christ into His death and raised to walk in newness of life. It is like putting on a team jersey in a sports contest. It tells everyone you are on Jesus' team.

Water baptism pictures spiritual baptism, a work of the Holy Spirit which takes place at salvation to all believers when they trust Christ. This is described in **1 Corinthians 12.**

12 "For even as the body is one and yet has many members, and all the members of the body, though they are many, are one body, so also is Christ. **13** For by one Spirit we were all baptized into one body, whether Jews or Greeks, whether slaves or free, and we were all made to drink of one Spirit." (1 Corinthians 12:12,13)

Water baptism is a perfect outward picture of what happens with Spirit baptism when we are plunged into the body of Christ. Water baptism is our outward way of testifying what has happened inside.

BAPTIZED INTO CHRIST BODY AND NOW DEAD TO SIN (6:3-7)

3 Or do you not know that all of us who have been baptized into Christ Jesus have been baptized into His death? **4** Therefore we have been buried with Him through baptism into death, so that as Christ was raised from the dead through the glory of the Father, so we too might walk in newness of life. **5** For if we have become united with *Him* in the likeness of His death, certainly we shall also be *in the likeness* of His resurrection, **6** knowing this, that our old self was crucified with *Him*, in order that our body of sin might be done away with, so that we would no longer be slaves to sin; **7** for he who has died is freed from sin.

Verse 3 teaches that we have been joined with Christ in his death. He died in our place on the cross. He didn't just die for us, He died <u>as us</u>.

"He made Him who knew no sin <u>to be sin</u> on our behalf, so that we might become the righteousness of God in Him." (2 Corinthians 5:21)

What an immense thought. He became our sin on the cross. The wrath of God, that we deserved, was poured out on Him instead

104

of us. When we trust in His finished work we become part of His life and His family, the Church.

Verses 4 and 5 continue. Now that we are baptized into His death, we are also identified with His resurrection. Being raised in newness of life, we need to live with Christ's power in our new life. In the same way, we are identified with the death and burial of Christ, so we are identified with the resurrection of Christ. When we are baptized in water we show the world what has happened to us. The words used during water baptism usually refer to being "baptized in the name of the Father, Son, and Holy Spirit, buried with Christ in baptism and raised to walk in newness of life."

Verses 6 and 7 focus on the victory over sin that comes with the new life in Christ. We have been crucified with Christ, who paid for all our sins and defeated our enemy, Satan. We are now no longer under the bondage of sin like we were before we came to Christ. Our old self was a slave to sin. Our new self has been emancipated, freed, from that bondage. When a person is dead, sin no longer has any authority over him. We have died with Christ and have been lifted up out of the swamp of sin and placed on solid ground. If the Son sets us free, we are free indeed to no longer choose sin. Does that mean we can no longer sin? No, it means we don't have to sin. We have God's resources to live in victory. **Chapter 7** will deal with this issue more in depth.

Alive to God in Christ (6:8-11)

8 Now if we have died with Christ, we believe that we shall also live with Him, **9** knowing that Christ, having been raised from the dead, is never to die again; death no longer is master over Him. **10** For the death that He died, He died to sin once for all; but the life that He lives, He lives to God. **11** Even so consider yourselves to be dead to sin, but alive to God in Christ Jesus.

The first seven verses focus primarily on the fact that the death of Christ frees us from the demands and constraints of sin. These next verses focus, not on death, but on life. It is logical. If we died with Christ, then it follows that we also were raised with Him. Christ will never die again and we will never again be under the mastery of sin. When He said it was "finished," it was. Jesus was obedient to the Father in His life all the way to the cross. We are now free to honor God with our lives. We now, as believers, can join with Paul:

> **"I have been crucified with Christ; and it is no longer I who live, but Christ lives in me; and the life which I now live in the flesh I live by faith in the Son of God, who loved me and gave Himself up for me."**
> (Galatians 2:20)

> **"For to me, to live is Christ and to die is gain."**
> (Philippians 1:*21)*

Rejecting sin as your master (6:12-14)

12 Therefore do not let sin reign in your mortal body so that you obey its lusts, **13** and do not go on presenting the members of your body to sin *as* instruments of unrighteousness; but present yourselves to God as those alive from the dead, and your members *as* instruments of righteousness to God. **14** For sin shall not be master over you, for you are not under law but under grace.

In light of all God has done for us, Paul pleads with believers to not return to the very sin Christ died to destroy. We have a new master in Christ and have been freed from our former master, sin.

106

He warns about continuing in sin, yielding our bodies over to the lusts of the flesh. We, instead, need to be constantly yielding our lives to God to be used for righteous works. We have the grace of God to strengthen us so we don't have to give in to the law of sin and death. Sin never needs to be our master. It now comes down to a choice. What will we yield to, sin, or the will of God?

Changing masters (6:15-19)

15 What then? Shall we sin because we are not under law but under grace? May it never be! **16** Do you not know that when you present yourselves to someone *as* slaves for obedience, you are slaves of the one whom you obey, either of sin resulting in death, or of obedience resulting in righteousness? **17** But thanks be to God that though you were slaves of sin, you became obedient from the heart to that form of teaching to which you were committed, **18** and having been freed from sin, you became slaves of righteousness. **19** I am speaking in human terms because of the weakness of your flesh. For just as you presented your members as slaves to impurity and to lawlessness, resulting in *further* lawlessness, so now present your members as slaves to righteousness, resulting in sanctification.

Paul uses the illustration of slaves and masters to teach us an important lesson. In the ancient world, slaves and masters were very common. There were different types of slavery. When nations were captured they were forced into slavery as a conquered people. They served the Roman Empire. There were also instances when a citizen found himself in difficult times and had to work off a debt. Paul uses this common part of society to describe a Christian's relationship with sin.

We are slaves to the one we choose to serve. It is as simple as that. We can choose to serve God or give in to the desires of the flesh and serve the enemy of our souls. Paul even tells them he is speaking in human terms **(verse 19)** because we all struggle with weakness in our flesh. Paul will develop that more in **Chapter 7**.

He points out that we were born in sin and slaves to our sinful nature. Christ changed all that. As believers, we are now no longer under the rule of sin and death. That was settled on the cross. Now, we have new freedom and can choose righteousness over sin. We could not do that before we came to Christ **(Romans 3:10-19).**

The challenge of this passage is that we are free to make choices. We should choose to follow righteousness instead of sin. Being under the grace of God is not a reason to presume that we are free to sin. We have been called to live as free men and women, to honor and serve God, not to continue in sin. We are now God's slaves, by choice, and He is the One we want to serve.

From a life leading to death to one leading to life (6:20-23)

20 For when you were slaves of sin, you were free in regard to righteousness. **21** Therefore what benefit were you then deriving from the things of which you are now ashamed? For the outcome of those things is death. **22** But now having been freed from sin and enslaved to God, you derive your benefit, resulting in sanctification, and the outcome, eternal life. **23** For the wages of sin is death, but the free gift of God is eternal life in Christ Jesus our Lord.

Paul begins by reminding them of the time when they were not part of God's family and were slaves to sin. He is asking them, "What kind of life was that? Did it do anything good for you? Why would you want to choose to go back into that kind of slavery when you can live in God's wonderful freedom? Why would you want to go back and do those things that you are ashamed of today?"

This passage is a clear formula. Being a slave to sin leads to death. Being a slave of righteousness leads to eternal life. Given those options, why would a child of God choose to go back to a dark path of carnality and walking in darkness? There is no benefit of any kind in that choice. There are instances in both the Old and New Testament where a person who was called as part of the family of God turned to his own way and physical death came as a judgment. Nadab and Abihu, the sons of Aaron, brought shame on the camp of Israel by ignoring the commands of God and suffered the wrath of God **(Leviticus 15)**. Jonah, likewise, learned that it is not a wise choice to ignore God's directives **(Jonah Chapters 1 and 2).** Ananias and Sapphira in the book of Acts tried to deceive the church and ended up being struck dead **(Acts 5)**. Others in the church in Corinth made a mockery of the Lord's supper and died. These and others have learned that the holiness and righteousness of God is not something to ignore.

> [23] **"For the wages of sin is death, but the free gift of God is eternal life in Christ Jesus our Lord."**

But one might ask, "I know this is all true, I really want to be living a life that honors God. But why do I have such a struggle with sin?"

That question brings us to chapter 7.

Romans 7

²⁴ "Wretched man that I am! Who will set me free from the body of this death?"

CHAPTER OVERVIEW

Previously, we were commanded to no longer present the members of our body to sin. We are a new creation and should not go back and do those things we formerly did that were shameful. Paul also reminds Jewish believers they were captive under the Law, but now are free from the old system which was fulfilled in Christ. For the believer, there is no going back. In a marriage when a spouse dies, the survivor can start over again, no longer under the old marriage contract. When Christ died, He ended the old marriage contract and a new one was established based on grace, not the Law.

The second half of **Romans 7** brings up the reality of the struggle of living a righteous life in an unrighteous world. The temptations and pressures of the world around us still appeal to our fleshly nature, even though we know in our spirit it is wrong to follow those primal lusts. We have a war inside. The spirit is willing, but the flesh is weak. It is real life. There is hope.

THE KEY VERSES FOR CHAPTER 7

⁵ "For while we were in the flesh, the sinful passions, which were aroused by the Law, were at work in the members of our body to bear fruit for death. ⁶ But now we have been released from the Law, having died to that by which we were bound, so that we serve in newness of the Spirit and not in oldness of the letter."

SIMPLE OUTLINE

I. Romans 7:1-6. Setting aside the old Law for the newness of the Spirit.

II. Romans 7:7-13. The purpose of the Law was to lead us to Christ.

III. Romans 7:14-25. The war within – The flesh and our spirit.

Romans 7 Commentary

Romans 7:1-6: Setting aside the old Law for the newness of the spirit.

1 Or do you not know, brethren (for I am speaking to those who know the law), that the law has jurisdiction over a person as long as he lives? **2** For the married woman is bound by law to her husband while he is living; but if her husband dies, she is released from the law concerning the husband. **3** So then, if while her husband is living she is joined to another man, she shall be called an adulteress; but if her husband dies, she is free from the law, so that she is not an adulteress though she is joined to another man.

4 Therefore, my brethren, you also were made to die to the Law through the body of Christ, so that you might be joined to another, to Him who was raised from the dead, in order that we might bear fruit for God. **5** For while we were in the flesh, the sinful passions, which were aroused by the Law, were at work in the members of our body to bear fruit for death. **6** But now we have been released from the Law, having died to that by which we were bound, so that we serve in newness of the Spirit and not in oldness of the letter.

UNDERSTANDING THE LAW - IMPORTANT THINGS WE NEED TO KNOW BEFORE LOOKING INTO THESE VERSES.

The first half of this chapter is directed to the Jewish believers living in Rome. Paul is reminding them that the Law which was given to them by God had a specific purpose. That purpose was to expose the sin of the people and ultimately lead them to embrace faith in God. No man was ever justified by keeping the Law, only by exercising faith. The death of Christ on the cross marked the end of the purpose of the Law. When Jesus said, "It is finished," He meant just that.

Everything God instituted in the Old Testament was designed to drive a man to repentance and find life in God through faith. The sacrifices, the temple, the priests, the feasts, the Law, all of it was a picture, or shadow of what was coming, the final sacrifice of God's Son for our sin.

> **"For the Law, since it has only a shadow of the good things to come and not the very form of things, can never, by the same sacrifices which they offer continually year by year, make perfect those who draw near."** (Hebrews 10:1)

When we discuss "the Law" in the New Testament times we are, in most cases, referring to the entire Old Testament system God established to not just protect His people from the pagan world, but to preserve them as a nation to fulfill their appointed task and privilege of bringing in the Messiah, the Savior of the world. When Jesus came, died and rose again, the purpose of the entire system was fulfilled, completed. As Jesus said, "It is finished." At His death, the veil in the temple was ripped, top to bottom, by the hand of God. The old system was over. When we talk about the Law, this is what we need to keep in mind. It is what Paul understood. He was formerly a Pharisee trying to be righteous by keeping all the details of the Law, but he ended up empty. When he came to faith in Christ, everything changed. It was all by grace, not by anything he had done.

Now, we can begin looking at **Chapter 7**.

THE ILLUSTRATION OF MARRIAGE

1 Or do you not know, brethren (for I am speaking to those who know the law), that the law has jurisdiction over a person as long as he lives? **2** For the married woman is bound by law to her husband while he is living; but if her husband dies, she is released from the law concerning the husband. **3** So then, if while her husband is living she is joined to another man, she shall be called an adulteress; but if her husband dies, she is free from the law, so that she is not an adulteress though she is joined to another man.

When a person marries, a vow is taken that the union of man and wife is to last as long as both partners are alive. At the death of one of the members, the vow of marriage is fulfilled, the covenant to remain together is nullified. Any intimate relationship that occurs outside of marriage while the two are still married is considered adultery. We understand these things as did the Jewish nation. Paul is reminding them that the marriage covenant is serious and lasts until one of the partners dies. He uses this illustration to explain the jurisdiction the Law has over a person and to make sure his listeners are all on the same page.

Then he proceeds to compare the principles of marriage to the Law of God.

TODAY, THE CEREMONIES AND LAW OF GOD ARE LIKE A SPOUSE THAT HAS DIED

4 "Therefore, my brethren, you also were made to die to the Law through the body of Christ, so that you might be joined to another, to Him who was raised from the dead, in order that we might bear fruit for God. **5** For while we were in the flesh, the sinful passions, which were aroused by the Law, were at work in the members of our body to bear fruit for death. **6** But now we have been released from the Law, having died to that by which we were bound, so that we serve in newness of the Spirit and not in oldness of the letter."

Verses 1-3 reminded the people that a wife was bound to her husband by covenant as long as the husband lived. When the husband died, she was no longer bound to that covenant, she was freed from the husband's authority and free to marry another.

The Law of God was given to Israel. It was a marriage covenant with its moral code (the 10 Commandments), its priests, sacrifices, and everything else associated with the nation of Israel. Israel was betrothed to God. Like marriage, it was to last until death. The ancient Rabbis used to teach that the only way a man could be free from the Law was to die. If a servant died, he was no longer under the rule of his master.

When Jesus died on the cross, the system was finished, it died. Jesus is the Messiah God promised, the One the Old Testament pointed to, the end of the Law. When He died, everything the Law was meant to accomplish was completed. Now, Paul is reminding the people that they are now dead to the Law and free to marry another **(Verse 4)**.

We don't need the old sacrificial system anymore, we have Christ Himself. We are now free to enter into covenant relationship with Him and that marriage, unlike the temporary one, does not have an expiration date.

In the Old Testament times, God gave the people pictures before He sent the Person. Now, the Person has come, we no longer need the pictures. The Law was the pictures. It is finished, Christ Himself has come.

Verse 5 helps explain that the Law exposed the sin in our hearts with the purpose of leading us to repentance and faith. The Law was like a prosecutor proving our guilt.

Have you ever seen a sign warning about wet paint? Before you saw the sign, you didn't know there was wet paint. What happens when you see the sign? Human nature cannot seem to resist touching the paint. The sign not only tells us the paint is wet but also proves how dumb we are when we touch the wet paint. The Law reveals that we have sinned and even, as **Verse 5** says, arouses our sinful passions and we sin more. All of this convinces us that we are sinners.

Verse 6 shows us that we are now free from the Law. The Holy Spirit has freed us from the constraints of the Law and leads us in newness of life. Our relationship with God is no longer based on a set of instructions, but a living relationship with God. The old priests and sacrifices are finished. Christ is our final High Priest and final sacrifice. We are in the family of God, no longer in bondage to the system of the Law. We live in newness of the Holy Spirit.

Paul continues in the next verses to explain in more detail about the Law and our relationship to it as believers. Even though these teachings are addressed to the Jewish believers, those given the Law, the principles were for the Gentile believers as well.

Romans 7:7-13: The purpose of the Law was to lead us to Christ.

7 What shall we say then? Is the Law sin? May it never be! On the contrary, I would not have come to know sin except through the Law; for I would not have known about cov-

eting if the Law had not said, "YOU SHALL NOT COVET." **8** But sin, taking opportunity through the commandment, produced in me coveting of every kind; for apart from the Law sin is dead. **9** I was once alive apart from the Law; but when the commandment came, sin became alive and I died; **10** and this commandment, which was to result in life, proved to result in death for me; **11** for sin, taking an opportunity through the commandment, deceived me and through it killed me. **12** So then, the Law is holy, and the commandment is holy and righteous and good.

13 Therefore did that which is good become a cause of death for me? May it never be! Rather it was sin, in order that it might be shown to be sin by effecting my death through that which is good, so that through the commandment sin would become utterly sinful.

HAVE YOU EVER WONDERED WHY WOULD GOD GIVE A LAW THAT NO MAN COULD KEEP?

The Law was good, yet it did not provide the power that we need to keep it. The Law exposed our sin. The beginning of true repentance and faith is first realizing we are desperate sinners, incapable of solving our problem. We need help. We need God. That is why God gave the Law that no man could keep. It revealed how Holy God is, how sinful we are and how we cannot save ourselves. The Law leads us to God where we find forgiveness and life. This is what **verse 7** teaches us, "I would not have come to know sin except through the Law; for I would not have known about coveting if the Law had not said, "YOU SHALL NOT COVET." Remember when Jesus told a rich young ruler that to find eternal life he needed to keep the Law? **Romans 7:7-13** will now shed light on that story. Let's review that encounter from **Mark.**

¹⁷ "As He was setting out on a journey, a man ran up to

Him and knelt before Him, and asked Him, "Good Teacher, what shall I do to inherit eternal life?" [18] And Jesus said to him, "Why do you call Me good? No one is good except God alone. [19] You know the commandments, 'DO NOT MURDER, DO NOT COMMIT ADULTERY, DO NOT STEAL, DO NOT BEAR FALSE WITNESS, Do not defraud, HONOR YOUR FATHER AND MOTHER.'" [20] And he said to Him, "Teacher, I have kept all these things from my youth up." [21] Looking at him, Jesus felt a love for him and said to him, "One thing you lack: go and sell all you possess and give to the poor, and you will have treasure in heaven; and come, follow Me." [22] But at these words, he was saddened, and he went away grieving, for he was one who owned much property." (Mark 10:17-22)

Before this young man met Jesus, things were going pretty well for him. At least he thought he was doing well. He felt God had blessed him since he was rich and influential. He had checked all the boxes in the Jewish Law and kept the commandments. In the eyes of Jewish society, the young man had it all together. When Jesus came down the road, the man showed humility in bowing before Him. His purpose, from what we can read in the text, was to justify his life and to be assured that he had done it all right. He tells Jesus that he had kept all the Law perfectly, since his youth. He wanted assurance that what he had done was enough to inherit eternal life.

What happens next is the most astonishing part of the story. Instead of Jesus telling the young man to just believe and follow Him, he says something shocking. He tells the young man to sell everything he has and give it away. Why? Was that in the Law Jesus just told the man to follow? Actually, yes. The Law is summed up by "love God and love your neighbor as you love yourself." If a person loved his neighbor as himself, he would not horde his riches. He would give them to his neighbor. Jesus is exposing the sin of the man by explaining what the Law really means. Once the young man was confronted with the real impact of the Law, he, for the first time, understood he had not kept the Law but was indeed a lost sinner. Before a person comes to faith, he must first understand he is lost in sin.

The Law, in essence, made him more sinful. This is what **verses 9 and 10** teach.

> [9] **"I was once alive apart from the Law; but when the commandment came, sin became alive and I died; 10 and this commandment, which was to result in life, proved to result in death for me."**

CANCER AND THE X-RAY

Think of a man who has cancer. He may feel fine and go about his daily life in a state of deceptive peace. One day, he has an x-ray at a hospital and malignant tumors are found throughout his body. He was a dead man before he found out the truth. He felt he was alive. When the x-ray exposed his cancer, he then understood for the first time he was a dead man walking. The Law is that x-ray. The Law is not bad but, to the man with cancer, it means death. That x-ray drives the man to seek a cure. The Law reveals our sin and drives us to Christ where there alone we find the cure.

Keeping the Law of God never brought life, but it exposed the depth of our sin and brought us into the realization of just how sinful we are. **Verse 12** asks, "Is the Law itself sinful?" It seems to make sin worse. The answer is in **verse 13**:

> [13] **"Therefore did that which is good become a cause of death for me? May it never be! Rather it was sin, in order that it might be shown to be sin by effecting my death through that which is good, so that through the commandment sin would become utterly sinful."**

The rich young ruler came to Jesus in arrogant self-righteousness. He went away in sorrow, seeing himself as a lost sinner.

That is what the moral Law does. The fact that he went away sorrowful is the hope in this story. We don't know what he did with his sin. The answer is to go back to Jesus this time as a sinner. He would find the eternal life he was seeking.

The rich young ruler, like the man who had cancer, was walking about each day with neither agitation or alarm that anything was wrong. He actually thought he was healthy. One day he met the Great Physician who took a look at the young ruler's x-ray and saw what the young ruler had not seen. He found cancer. The young man had indeed broken all the Law. He had not loved God and his neighbor as he loved himself. If he had, then he would have shared all he had with his neighbor instead of keeping it all for himself. The Law indeed exposed just how advanced the cancer was. He left very different than he came. He left informed of the truth. The sad part is that the One who read his spiritual x-ray was indeed the Great Physician and had the cure for his cancer of sin. It is not revealed if the young man ever went back for a second office visit.

Now we come to the final section of this chapter. When a person believes in Jesus and has his sins forgiven, does that mean he no longer has to deal with sin? That is the next topic Paul tackles.

Romans 7:14-25. The war within – The flesh and the spirit.

14 For we know that the Law is spiritual, but I am of flesh, sold into bondage to sin. **15** For what I am doing, I do not understand; for I am not practicing what I would like to do, but I am doing the very thing I hate. **16** But if I do the very thing I do not want to do, I agree with the Law, confessing that the Law is good. **17** So now, no longer am I the one doing it, but sin which dwells in me. **18** For I know that nothing good dwells in me, that is, in my flesh; for the willing is present in me, but the doing of the good is not. **19** For the good that I want, I do not do, but I practice the very evil that I do not want. **20** But if I am doing the very thing I do not want, I am no longer the one doing it, but sin which dwells in me.

21 I find then the principle that evil is present in me, the one who wants to do good. **22** For I joyfully concur with the law of God in the inner man, **23** but I see a different law in the members of my body, waging war against the law of my mind and making me a prisoner of the law of sin which is in my members. **24** Wretched man that I am! Who will set me free from the body of this death? **25** Thanks be to God through Jesus Christ our Lord! So then, on the one hand I myself with my mind am serving the law of God, but on the other, with my flesh the law of sin.

THE FLESH

"The things that please and gratify our senses and animal appetites and passions, or our corrupt nature, namely, things visible and temporal; the things of the earth, such as pleasure, (of sense or imagination,) the praise of men, or the riches of this world," **(Benson commentary)**

"The rebellious human nature, human value systems that stand in opposition to God's value system. Here flesh is 'the body which is dominated by sin' ... the unregenerate and sinful state. The NIV nearly consistently translates this meaning of flesh as 'sinful nature.' Paul teaches that the fallen human nature is inherently rebellious against God. We inherited this nature from Adam and, unfortunately, it was not eradicated when we became Christians. It is still within us, but we are no longer forced to follow its dictates." **(Dr. Ralph Wilson)**

Galatians 5 tells us what the flesh produces in our lives.

> **"The acts of the sinful nature (the flesh) are obvious: sexual immorality, impurity, and debauchery; idolatry and witchcraft; hatred, discord, jealousy, fits of rage, selfish ambition, dissensions, factions, and envy; drunkenness, orgies, and the like."** (Galatians 5:19-21)

Wars rage all around us today. Country against country, neighbor against neighbor, husband against wife. And we are at war within ourselves, our flesh battles our spirit. It is a world of turmoil, all because of the fall of man.

IMPORTANT BACKGROUND FOR THIS PASSAGE

This passage has a fair amount of controversy associated with it. There are basically three major views and several variations under each of the three. Theologians throughout the centuries differ on their positions. The following are basic views:

1. Paul is describing the struggle of all believers.

2. Paul is describing the state of an unbeliever, including his own struggle before he was converted.

3. Paul is describing humanity in general, neither saved nor unsaved. It is a human condition from the fall.

All views acknowledge that a struggle with sin exists. Some think a person can achieve sinless perfection in this life, but most reject that idea.

I lean toward position one and feel that Paul was describing his own personal struggle. At the same time, I acknowledge that there are many students of the Word that hold different views. As we look at this, let's consider the main point where there is general agreement. All of mankind is in a struggle with sin.

Paul certainly considered himself as a sinner even though redeemed:

> [12] "I thank Christ Jesus our Lord, who has strengthened me, because He considered me faithful, putting me into service, [13] even though I was formerly a blasphemer and a persecutor and a violent aggressor. Yet I was shown mercy because I acted ignorantly in unbelief; [14] and the grace of our Lord was more than abundant, with the faith and love which are found in Christ Jesus. [15] It is a trustworthy statement, deserving full acceptance, that Christ Jesus came into the world to save sinners, among whom I am foremost of all. [16] Yet for this reason I found mercy, so that in me as the foremost, Jesus Christ might demonstrate His perfect patience as an example for those who would believe in Him for eternal life." (1 Timothy 1:12-16)

Paul did not say he **was** a sinner, but that he **is** a sinner. He is saying he is a redeemed sinner in a carnal body. The flesh wars against the Spirit of God who indwells the believer. John shows us that it is an ongoing struggle. We never get to the point when we can say, "we have no sin."

8 "If we say that we have no sin, we are deceiving ourselves and the truth is not in us. **9** If we confess our sins, He is faithful and righteous to forgive us our sins and to cleanse us from all unrighteousness. **10** If we say that we have not sinned, we make Him a liar and His word is not in us."
(1 John 1:8-10)

It is not just the reality of indwelling sin that is important in this text. It is also critical to understand where the war is taking place.

THE WAR ZONE – BODY, SOUL, AND SPIRIT

"Now may the God of peace Himself sanctify you entirely; and may your spirit and soul and body be preserved complete, without blame at the coming of our Lord Jesus Christ." (1 Thessalonians 5:23)

12 "For the word of God is living and active and sharper than any two-edged sword, and piercing as far as the division of soul and spirit, of both joints and marrow, and able to judge the thoughts and intentions of the heart."
(Hebrews 4:12)

We realize we are made up of both material and non-material parts. We are both body or physical, and soul or spiritual. Yet everything is connected. We are one complete person. Because we can't see the non-physical part of us, we have to rely on what God tells us. We can't see the spiritual world or God with our physical eyes. No matter how much we learn, there is still a great mystery concerning the unseen world.

The two verses above tell us several things. We learn we are body, soul, and spirit. We also learn that the difference between soul and spirit is difficult to understand and only the Word of

God can separate the two. The illustration is given of bone and marrow in the physical body. Marrow is inside of bones and is actually the life of the body, producing blood cells. Yet the bones and marrow together make up the bones or skeletal system of the body. We may not be able to understand much else other than the two are one and yet separate in function.

Other passages in Scripture, when added together, give us more of the picture of how we are made. In the end, there are still some mysteries. Having said that, let me try to explain, in my limited knowledge, some general concepts about the body, soul, and spirit.

We live in a physical world. Our body is the vehicle we use to navigate the physical world. We use our senses like sight, touch, smell, hearing, and taste to connect with our world and each other. That is the part we can see. Words like emotion, heart, thought, conscience, understanding, love, will, choice, and others are not physical but affect our physical bodies. These human qualities are what we call the soul. The soul is in essence who we are.

Our physical body is the vehicle to connect us with the physical world and with each other. Using that analogy, the spirit is the spiritual vehicle to connect us with God.

When God created man, He made the body out of clay. He then breathed life into man, and man became a living soul. Mankind was made with the capacity to connect with others around him and his physical world. A part of the soul of man is called spirit. That part has the capacity to connect with God. When man fell into sin, all of man was damaged. We lie, steal, and kill our fellow man. We lost our connection to God.

When a person is saved, he is born of the Spirit. The spirit of man is reconnected to God. That reconnection to our Creator, the vertical connection begins to affect the horizontal connections with our neighbors and our world. Unfortunately, the flesh, the part of the soul that connects with our world still remains and is in tension with our spirit. The Holy Spirit indwells our human spirit but the flesh often wars against the Spirit. That is the tension we read about in **Romans 7**.

Here is how the Amplified Bible describes the new birth of the spirit

> [9] "No one who is born of God [deliberately, knowingly, and habitually] practices sin, because God's seed [His principle of life, the essence of His righteous character] remains [permanently] in him [who is born again—who is reborn from above—spiritually transformed, renewed, and set apart for His purpose]; and he [who is born again] cannot habitually [live a life characterized by] sin, because he is born of God and longs to please Him."
> (1 John 3:9 Amplified Bible)

In **Romans 7:16-23**, Paul describes the struggle between his spirit and his flesh, or fallen soul part, where sin continues to dwell. Lets re-read Paul's description of the war inside between the flesh and his spirit.

> [16] "But if I do the very thing I do not want to do, I agree with the Law, confessing that the Law is good. [17] So now, no longer am I the one doing it, but sin which dwells in me. [18] For I know that nothing good dwells in me, that is, in my flesh; for the willing is present in me, but the doing of the good is not. [19] For the good that I want, I do not do, but I practice the very evil that I do not want. [20] But if I am doing the very thing I do not want, I am no longer the one doing it, but sin which dwells in me. [21] I find then the principle that evil is present in me, the one who wants to do good. [22] For I joyfully concur with the law of God in the inner man, [23] but I see a different law in the members of my

body, waging war against the law of my mind and making me a prisoner of the law of sin which is in my members." (Romans 7:16-23)

No matter how we try to explain these things, we fall short. One thing we can be sure of is that our spirit is willing but our flesh is weak. And these two things are different from one another. Only God can divide the two as we saw in **Hebrews 4:12**. This is a continual war we will fight while on this earth. Should we lose heart? Never! There is hope that God will lead us to daily victories and ultimate victory.

> **"Therefore, we do not lose heart, but though our outer man is decaying, yet our inner man is being renewed day by day."** (2 Corinthians 4:16)

It is our time with God in His Word that will change us day by day.

And if you want to be really encouraged, keep reading.

Chapter 8 is just a page away and just may be the most encouraging and exciting news for believers found in the entire Bible.

Romans 8
Freedom

"Therefore there is now no condemnation for those who are in Christ Jesus"

CHAPTER OVERVIEW

I think Ray Pritchard pretty much sums up **Romans Chapter 8**:

> **"Romans 8 is the greatest chapter of the greatest book in the Bible!"**

This is a chapter of celebration. What a celebration it is! **Romans 8** is certainly one of the most beloved chapters in all of Scripture. It begins with no condemnation in Christ and ends with no chance of ever being condemned by Christ. Hope flows like a river and grace floods our souls. We left **Chapter 7** with the realization that we are deeply broken inside. The struggle with sin is a real burden. We find a God who not only understands the difficulties of life's journey but holds us tight and loves us unconditionally and eternally.

What begins with "no condemnation," wonderfully ends with no separation! It is no wonder that so many consider this their favorite chapter in all the Bible.

THE KEY VERSES FOR CHAPTER 8

[1] "Therefore there is now no condemnation for those who are in Christ Jesus. [2] For the law of the Spirit of life in Christ Jesus has set you free from the law of sin and of death."

SIMPLE OUTLINE

I. Romans 8:1-17. Setting aside the old Law for the newness of the Spirit.

II. Romans 8: 18-25. The end of the curse is coming.

III. Romans 8:26-39. We are held securely in the hands of God.

Romans 8 Commentary

Romans 8:1-17: Setting aside the old Law for the newness of the Spirit.

1 Therefore there is now no condemnation for those who are in Christ Jesus. **2** For the law of the Spirit of life in Christ Jesus has set you free from the law of sin and of death. **3** For what the Law could not do, weak as it was through the flesh, God *did*: sending His own Son in the likeness of sinful flesh and *as an offering* for sin, He condemned sin in the flesh, **4** so that the requirement of the Law might be fulfilled in us, who do not walk according to the flesh but according to the Spirit. **5** For those who are according to the flesh set their minds on the things of the flesh, but those who are according to the Spirit, the things of the Spirit. **6** For the mind set on the flesh is death, but the mind set on the Spirit is life and peace, **7** because the mind set on the flesh is hostile toward God; for it does not subject itself to the law of God, for it is not even able *to do so*, **8** and those who are in the flesh cannot please God.

(8:1) "Therefore" – no condemnation

Verse one uses the word "therefore." It can appear confusing. The previous chapter ends with our struggle with sin. Our flesh wars with our spirit (even Paul admits that he at times did the very thing he hated). Why would **Chapter 8** begin with "there is **therefore** now no condemnation?" If we wrote **verse one** we would be tempted to write, "Therefore because we sometimes fail as believers, we stand condemned before our holy God."

The word "therefore" is really referring back to the bigger story of the first seven chapters. Think back about that story. Man is desperately trapped in sin and helpless to solve his problem **(Chapters 1-3)**. Abraham helps us to understand no man can be made right with God by good works, religion, circumcision or baptism. Only faith can bring a man into a right relationship with God. We are pardoned (justified) by faith alone. It is a provision and work of God **(Chapters 3 and 5)**. When God saves us and adopts us into His family. He breaks the chains of sin which have held our soul captive and frees us forever. It is all a work of God, a result of His abundant grace **(Chapter 6)**.

We have the power of God and His strength available to us. Our souls have been freed from the mastery of sin. We still have our flesh and our sin nature waging war with our spirit. Yes, even as Christians we struggle with sin, but God does not abandon us. He provides help through our struggles **(Chapter 7).** With that in mind, Paul now begins **Chapter 8**:

> **"Therefore there is now no condemnation for those who are in Christ Jesus."**

We have been declared righteous, justified by God. **Justification is not based on our performance, but on our position "in Christ."** **Chapter 8** will be very clear that our position in Christ will never change. It is a work of God, not a work of man. It endures forever.

> **"The Christian's war with sin does not end until he goes to be with the Lord. Nevertheless, there is still no condemnation-because the penalty for all the failures of this life (and who of us does not have many, yea, even many every day!) has been paid in full at Calvary."** (Dr. Harry Ironside)

"The Law condemns, but the believer has a new relationship to the Law, and therefore he cannot be condemned."
(Warren Wiersbe)

"Therefore having been justified by faith, we have peace with God through our Lord Jesus Christ" (Romans 5:1)

Maybe it was thoughts like these that inspired the hymn writer to pen these words:

"I stand amazed in the presence
of Jesus, the Nazarene,
and wonder how he could love me,
a sinner, condemned, unclean."
(My Savior's Love by Charles H. Gabriel)

When Jesus saved you, He didn't say He would take away all your problems. He took away your condemnation.

[8:2-6]. TWO TYPES OF PEOPLE

This section compares two types of people. The one lives by the flesh, and the other is filled with God's Spirit. He has been given the spiritual resources to live victoriously, no longer having to obey the flesh. Before our salvation, we were under the authority of the law of sin and death. Once justified, we now are under the law of the spirit of life in Christ Jesus **(verse 2).**

We were condemned by the Law and were slaves of sin before conversion. When Christ died on the cross He bore our condemnation in His own body. The wages of our sin is death. Christ settled all the charges against us. Now, as free men, we can walk according to the Spirit. **(Verses 3 and 4)**

Today, there are those who choose to follow the ways of the flesh. However, we set our minds on the ways of God. Those who choose the flesh choose death. They must pay the penalty of the broken Law themselves. We who are of the Spirit, find life and peace **(verses 5 and 6).**

Those who choose to live their lives pursuing sin, and the desires of the flesh, can never please God **(verses 7 and 8)**

8:9-17 - What it means to be a child of God, to be "in the Spirit."

9 However, you are not in the flesh but in the Spirit, if indeed the Spirit of God dwells in you. But if anyone does not have the Spirit of Christ, he does not belong to Him. **10** If Christ is in you, though the body is dead because of sin, yet the spirit is alive because of righteousness. **11** But if the Spirit of Him who raised Jesus from the dead dwells in you, He who raised Christ Jesus from the dead will also give life to your mortal bodies through His Spirit who dwells in you.

12 So then, brethren, we are under obligation, not to the flesh, to live according to the flesh— **13** for if you are living according to the flesh, you must die; but if by the Spirit you are putting to death the deeds of the body, you will live. **14** For all who are being led by the Spirit of God, these are sons of God. **15** For you have not received a spirit of slavery leading to fear again, but you have received a spirit of adoption as sons by which we cry out, "Abba! Father!" **16** The Spirit Himself testifies with our spirit that we are children of God, **17** and if children, heirs also, heirs of God and fellow heirs with Christ, if indeed we suffer with *Him* so that we may also be glorified with *Him*.

OVERVIEW **Verses 2-8** described two types of people, those living according to the flesh and those living by the Spirit. In **verses 9-17,** Paul explains what life is like for the one living by the Spirit.

Verse 9 — Paul begins with the fact of the Indwelling work of the Spirit and our position in God's family. We belong to Him, and the Spirit of God lives in our lives. Other Scriptures describe this work of the Spirit as "sealing."

> **"The sealing of which Paul speaks here refers to an official mark of identification that was placed on a letter, contract, or another important document. The seal usually was made from hot wax, which was placed on the document and then impressed with a signet ring. The document was thereby officially identified with and under the authority of the person to whom the signet belonged.**
>
> **That is the idea behind our being sealed in Him [Christ] with the Holy Spirit of promise. The seal of God's Spirit in the believer signifies four primary things: security, authenticity, ownership, and authority."**
> (John MacArthur commenting on Romans 8:9 and Ephesians 1:13, 14)
>
> **"You were sealed in Him with the Holy Spirit of promise, who is given as a pledge of our inheritance"** (Ephesians 1:13–14)

Verses 10,11 — Paul assures us that even though our bodies are dead in sin, our spirit is alive through faith in Christ. We remain justified, declared righteous, because of the death and resurrection of Christ. The Spirit who raised Christ from the dead brings life to our damaged mortal bodies. Our righteousness is based on the Son of God. It is that righteousness that God sees when He looks at His children, no matter what flaws they have. What a great truth!

Verses 12-14 — Before we came to Christ, we only had one option, that was to sin. **Romans 3** was clear that no clean thing can be found in a lost man. The lost man does not seek God and is unable to do so. **Romans 8:12** tells us we are no longer under the rule of sin. We are now free to turn from it. **Romans 8:13 and 14** show that overcoming the flesh is a sign of true salvation. We can't honor God by living lives as we did before, continuing in sin. Through God's power we are able to turn from sin. This is what **Romans 8:13** is describing, "For all who are being led by the Spirit of God, these are sons of God." Remember King David? He had some serious flaws in his life but his heart for God is never questioned.

Verse 15 — We used to live in fear. Sin is a ruthless taskmaster. However, in Christ, we have been emancipated from our former slavery to sin. As adopted children, we have the same family love and privilege as true-born sons. We even call God the tender family name used by a true son, "Abba" or "Daddy." We are a family.

Verse 16 — The Holy Spirit also assures us of our place in God's family. He communicates with our spirit, assuring us of His presence and that we are, in fact, children of God. Before we were saved, if someone asked us if we knew for certain we were going to Heaven, we could only say, "I hope so." After we are born of the Spirit, we can now say, "Yes!" We don't say it because we have been taught to say it, but because deep inside we absolutely know it is true. That alone takes away our fears. This will be developed further in the last part of this chapter which ends with the promise, "If God is for us, who can stand against us?" (Romans 8:31).

Verse 17— There is enough in this one verse to preach or teach more than one lesson. Allow me to briefly mention three immense thoughts that come from this verse.

WE ARE HEIRS OF GOD AND CHRIST. Think what it means to be an heir. Imagine what it would mean to be the child of a king of a great country. Christ is King of kings. He will rule the world. He owns all things in the universe. We are His adopted child, part of the family of the King of kings. Remember what the father said to the elder brother in the prodigal son parable?

> 31 **"And he said to him, 'Son, you have always been with me, and all that is mine is yours."** (Luke 15:31)

We know the prodigal story is a picture of our loving Father. If God is infinite in riches, power, knowledge, love, and all His other attributes, and He says everything He has is ours, just how much is that? We are joint heirs with God and Christ. We can't even begin to imagine what is coming.

WE HAVE THE PRIVILEGE OF SUFFERING FOR HIS NAME. We don't often consider suffering to be a joy. However, in **James 1:2** we are told to "Consider it all joy, my brethren when you encounter various trials." When Jesus addressed the crowd in His sermon on the mount, He said:

> 10 **"Blessed are those who have been persecuted for the sake of righteousness, for theirs is the kingdom of heaven.** 11 **"Blessed are you when people insult you and persecute you, and falsely say all kinds of evil against you because of Me.** 12 **Rejoice and be glad, for your reward in heaven is great; for in the same way they persecuted the prophets who were before you."** (Matthew 5:10-12)

There are many benefits for those worthy to suffer for Christ. They are blessed. Theirs is the Kingdom of Heaven. Their reward in Heaven is **GREAT**. I made that word bold for a reason. Have you ever thought that the God who created the entire universe called it "good" after His work was done? This same

Creator says of those who suffer for Him that their reward is "**GREAT**." If God calls something "**GREAT**," then just how unimaginable is that?

WE WILL BE GLORIFIED WITH HIM. If the first two points are out of our range of understanding, then this one is also. The infinite glory of God cannot even be defined. It is related to His Holiness. Here is how one theologian defines holiness and glory.

> "Holiness is what He is as God that nobody else is. It is his quality of perfection that can't be improved upon, that can't be imitated, that is incomparable, that determines all that He is and is determined by nothing from outside Him. It signifies his infinite worth, his intrinsic, infinite worth, his intrinsic, infinite value." (John Piper)

Holiness is not something we can see. It is what God is by nature.

Glory is what we do see. It is the holiness of God manifested or made visible. We see this in **Isaiah 6:3**

> [3] "And one called out to another and said,
> "Holy, Holy, Holy, is the Lord of hosts,
> The whole earth is full of His glory."

We find in **Ephesians 5** what it means that we will be glorified as believers.

> [25] "Husbands, love your wives, just as Christ also loved the church and gave Himself up for her, [26] so that He might sanctify her, having cleansed her by the washing of water with the word, [27] that He might present to Himself the church in all her glory, having no spot or wrinkle or any such thing; but that she would be holy and blameless."
> (Ephesians 5:25-27)

It is Christ Himself who is glorious in nature, not us. We are in the process of being conformed into His image and in that way, we are glorified in Him. Jesus' greatest desire for His disciples was for them to see Him in his glory and be with Him. Listen to His prayer to the Father in **John 17**.

> [20] "I do not ask on behalf of these alone, but for those also who believe in Me through their word; [21] that they may all be one; even as You, Father, are in Me and I in You, that they also may be in Us, so that the world may believe that You sent Me.
> [22] The glory which You have given Me I have given to them, that they may be one, just as We are one; [23] I in them and You in Me, that they may be perfected in unity, so that the world may know that You sent Me, and loved them, even as You have loved Me. [24] Father, I desire that they also, whom You have given Me, be with Me where I am, so that they may see My glory which You have given Me, for You loved Me before the foundation of the world."
> (John 17:20-24)

For all pastors and teachers: Before we leave this section, **Romans 8:1-17**, I want to include three additional preaching and teaching outlines of this section.

OUTLINE NUMBER ONE

OUR HOPE - from **Romans 8:1-17**

Verse 1. We never face condemnation again.

Verse 2. We have the hope of being victors over the struggle with the flesh, our ever-present sin nature.

Verse 3-5. We are delivered from the requirements and constraints of the Law.

Verse 6-8. We have the hope of life and peace now and forever.

Verse 9. We have the promise, benefits, and the hope of the indwelling Holy Spirit and of our position in Christ.

Verses 10-11. We have a guaranteed hope that our bodies will one day be resurrected and never again face the contamination of sin and curse.

Verse 12-14. As declared sons of God, we are assured of continuing family relationship and knowing true life, which is found only in God.

Verse 15. Our family relationship with God the Father is very intimate, even closer than the best human relationship.

Verse 16-17. We have the hope of the Holy Spirit guaranteeing our place in God's family.

OUTLINE NUMBER TWO

Did you know that the word "Spirit" occurs some 20 times in **Romans 8** and that does not include the pronoun "Who"?

Promises that the Holy Spirit provides for every believer found in Romans 8

- **Freedom** (8:2)
- **Strength for service** (8:11)
- **Victory over sin** (8:13)
- **Guidance** (8:14)
- **The witness of sonship** (8:16)
- **Assistance in prayer** (8:26)

OUTLINE NUMBER THREE

Works of the Trinity in redemption found in Romans 8

Each member of the Trinity is involved in our redemption.
God the Father (verses 1, 3, 11, 14-16, 17)
God the Son (verses 1, 2, 3-4, 9, 10, 15-17)
God the Holy Spirit (verses 2, 4, 5-6, 9, 11, 13, 14, 15, 16)

Romans 8: 18-25. The End of the Curse is Coming

THE CURSE

The Fall of Man is recorded in Genesis chapter 3. The effects are felt to this day. Mankind was separated from the Creator. Death and decay entered the creation. God cursed man, animals, plants, everything. Depravity saturated what was once a pristine and beautiful work of art, a glorious universe. **Romans 8:22** declares that because of the curse, *"all creation groans ..."* Every inch of the universe has been impacted by the curse God put on His broken world. It was damaged by the rebellious sin of man. But one day, the curse will be removed, all things made new. A new Heaven and new earth will glorify God as was once intended. Jesus bore the curse in His own body on the cross. The ultimate effects of His resurrection will one day be seen in the great resurrection when all things are made new. What man broke, Jesus paid for, and God will restore. Every inch of the cursed universe, and the hurting hearts of the children of God anxiously await that great day.

18 For I consider that the sufferings of this present time are not worthy to be compared with the glory that is to be revealed to us. **19** For the anxious longing of the creation waits eagerly for the revealing of the sons of God. **20** For the creation was subjected to futility, not willingly, but because of Him who subjected it, in hope **21** that the creation itself also will be set free from its slavery to corruption into the freedom of the glory of the children of God. **22** For we know that the whole creation groans and suffers the pains of childbirth together until now. **23** And not only this, but also we ourselves, having the first fruits of the Spirit, even we ourselves groan within ourselves, waiting eagerly for *our* adoption as sons, the redemption of our body. **24** For in hope we have been saved, but hope that is seen is not hope; for who hopes for what he *already* sees? **25** But if we hope for what we do not see, with perseverance we wait eagerly for it.

*IMPORTANT BACKGROUND QUESTION TO ANSWER BEFORE WE LOOK AT THIS PASSAGE.

IF GOD IS GOOD WHY DOES HE ALLOW SUFFERING IN THE WORLD?

This is not a new question. It is considered the most common concern people have in the world today who are struggling to believe in God. The following is how the Greek philosopher Epicurus phrased the question in 300 BC:

> "If God wants to abolish evil, and cannot, He is impotent.
> If He can, but does not want to, he is wicked.
> But If God both can and wants to abolish evil, then how come evil is in the world?"

Epicurus concluded that God cannot exist. Scientist Charles

Darwin, and philosopher Bertrand Russell, came to the same conclusion. They struggled with this question. It is important for all pastors and teachers to understand how to answer those who seek to know **"How can God be loving when there is evil in the world?"**

These are the basic points that need to be understood to answer this important question.

FIRST — God is love and everything He created was beautiful and perfect.

> [8] **The one who does not love does not know God, for God is love.** (1 John 4:8)

SECOND — When God created man, He created him as a free being. This was a requirement of love.

1 Corinthians 13:4-8 describes how love acts, which helps us understand how God acts.

> [4] **"Love is patient, love is kind and is not jealous; love does not brag and is not arrogant,** [5] **does not act unbecomingly; it does not seek its own, is not provoked, does not take into account a wrong suffered,** [6] **does not rejoice in unrighteousness, but rejoices with the truth;** [7]**bears all things, believes all things, hopes all things, endures all things.**[8] **Love never fails."**

What this tells us about God is that Creation was an act of love. God made something outside of Himself, not because He needed it. He needed nothing. He did it to share and that is love. Also, we learn that the creation had to be free. Man was not created as a robot. Love requires choice and decision. A robot can be programmed to say "I love you." That is not really love. Remember, love does not demand its way. Love is a choice, so God made the human race with the gift of free choice. He loves us and wants us to love Him. We also see that God is patient and endures all the failings of a free creation. And that is what Jesus did on the cross, He endured the sins of the fallen creation to the point of death. Why? Because God so loved the world that He gave His son.

THIRD — Suffering and evil are not the direct creation of God. They are the product of the disobedience of man, a free creature, who chose to go his own way. God allowed His free creation to go the way it chose even when there were adequate warnings of the consequences. God is patient and endures all things.

FOURTH — To take away all evil and suffering in the world, which are caused by sin, God would have to take away free will but He can't do that since love does not demand its own way. Man had to be free for love to exist. Sin and suffering will always be with us until the day when the curse is removed, and a new Heaven and earth begin **(Revelation 21 and 22)**.

FIFTH — Jesus' death on the cross was the greatest act of love in the history of the universe. He became sin for us **(2 Corinthians 5:21)**. He bore the curse on the cross.

> **"Christ redeemed us from the curse of the Law, having become a curse for us—for it is written, "Cursed is everyone who hangs on a tree"** (Galatians 3:13).

Conclusion – How can God be loving if there is evil and suffering in the world? Evil and suffering are in the world because God is loving. He, out of love and patience, allowed His creation to be free enough to reject Him, and they did. That rejection, which Love allowed, brought on the consequences God warned would happen. Death and curse entered His spotless creation. God sent His Son to fix it all. He died so that death would not be

143

our final destination. He became the curse and bore the wrath of God in our place. Now, everyone who follows Him are forgiven, and will one day be united with Him forever in a curse-free universe in curse-free resurrected bodies. Remember, the curse is only temporary.

Epicurus was wrong. God is neither impotent nor unloving.

Now we can proceed to **Romans 8:18-25**.

Romans 8: 18-25. The End of the Curse is Coming

Two major themes run throughout this passage

- The curse on the universe and the sufferings of all men, including believers, are the result of the fall of man.

- A future glory is promised for all of God's redeemed children.

Romans 8:18-25 is an incredible scene describing the creation of God in absolute agony bearing the excruciating weight of the curse. The creation groans, aches, suffers, and wails. It is seen in the animal world where death and misery are everywhere. Plants endure thorns, rot, mildew, and harmful pests, just struggling to stay alive. Death stalks life. All of creation was created in love and care. It was designed to glorify God and know freedom and beauty. Now everything dies. Winds and floods, fires and brutal weather pound the earth relentlessly. Stars explode and burn up. The universe is at war and losing. We are in the middle of the storm and affected by all of it. Animals created to be our friends are now our enemies. Work was created to honor God, designed to be fulfilling, but now we work hard just to eat.

144

We are at odds with our neighbors, nations are against nations. It is all wrong, all broken. The universe is in agony hoping that one day the misery will end. We want a world where we will never again have to say "Good-bye." In our minds, we know that something is coming, something better. It is!

22 For we know that the whole creation groans and suffers the pains of childbirth together until now. **23** And not only this, but also, we ourselves, having the first fruits of the Spirit, even we ourselves groan within ourselves, waiting eagerly for *our* adoption as sons, the redemption of our body.

Verse 23 says we have the "first fruits of the Spirit." The Jewish feast of First Fruits was a required festival **(Leviticus 23)** when the people of God offered the first of their crops to the Lord as a pledge of their faith and hope that God would bring in the full harvest. Fifty days later, the feast of Pentecost was the celebration of the great harvests. The Holy Spirit has sealed us into His family and is our pledge of the coming great harvest. He is our first fruits pledge. He sealed and adopted us into the family of God and is our guarantee that the fullness of our salvation will be realized one day when the great harvest is complete. All of God's children will be safe in His arms when the roll call is complete. Yes, something wonderful is coming.

18 For I consider that the sufferings of this present time are not worthy to be compared with the glory that is to be revealed to us. **19** For the anxious longing of the creation waits eagerly for the revealing of the sons of God.

When that day comes

> [3] "And I heard a loud voice from the throne, saying, "Behold, the tabernacle of God is among men, and He will

145

dwell among them, and they shall be His people, and God Himself will be among them, [4] and He will wipe away every tear from their eyes; and there will no longer be any death; there will no longer be any mourning, or crying, or pain; the first things have passed away."(Revelation 21:3, 4)

That day is a great hope for all who have trusted Christ. This chapter is not over yet. There is much more hope ahead in the closing section, **Romans 8:26-39**.

Romans 8:26-39. We are Held Securely in the Hands of God

26 In the same way the Spirit also helps our weakness; for we do not know how to pray as we should, but the Spirit Himself intercedes for us with groanings too deep for words; **27** and He who searches the hearts knows what the mind of the Spirit is, because He intercedes for the saints according to the will of God.

28 And we know that God causes all things to work together for good to those who love God, to those who are called according to His purpose. **29** For those whom He foreknew, He also predestined to become conformed to the image of His Son, so that He would be the firstborn among many brethren; **30** and these whom He predestined, He also called; and these whom He called, He also justified; and these whom He justified, He also glorified.

31 What then shall we say to these things? If God is for us, who is against us? **32** He who did not spare His own Son, but delivered Him over for us all, how will He not also with Him freely give us all things? **33** Who will bring a charge against God's elect? God is the one who justifies; **34** who is the one who condemns? Christ Jesus is He who died, yes, rather who was raised, who is at the right hand of God, who also intercedes for us. **35** Who will separate us from the love of Christ? Will tribulation, or distress, or persecution, or famine, or nakedness, or peril, or sword? **36** Just as it is written,

> "For Your sake we are being put to death all day long;
> We were considered as sheep to be slaughtered."

37 But in all these things we overwhelmingly conquer through Him who loved us. **38** For I am convinced that neither death, nor life, nor angels, nor principalities, nor things present, nor things to come, nor powers, **39** nor height, nor depth, nor any other created thing, will be able to separate us from the love of God, which is in Christ Jesus our Lord.

Of all the passages in the Bible, this may be the most precious, most reassuring, and most hopeful of them all. It is all about God. It demonstratres that He is our powerful and unchanging God. We can be certain we are safe, secure, certain, hopeful and a thousand other things. These are the words of the living God and will stand forever **(Isaiah 40:8)**

ROMANS 8:26,27 - THE HOLY SPIRIT INTERCEDES FOR US

26 In the same way the Spirit also helps our weakness; for we do not know how to pray as we should, but the Spirit Himself intercedes for *us* with groanings too deep for words; **27** and He who searches the hearts knows what the mind of the Spirit is, because He intercedes for the saints according to *the will of* God.

Even believers can be overwhelmed, running out of words to say. We can be discouraged, beaten down, frustrated with people and things. There is One who understands our weaknesses and carries our needs to the throne of God. Jesus said He would send a helper and He did.

> **"I will ask the Father, and He will give you another Helper, that He may be with you forever;**
> **But the Helper, the Holy Spirit, whom the Father will send in My name, He will teach you all things, and bring to your remembrance all that I said to you."** (John 14:16, 26)

For the unbeliever, there are fewer things more terrifying than the thought that God knows all about us. For the believer, it is a great comfort that God knows everything about His children and loves and cares for each of our individual needs. Nobody can pray and intercede for us better than the Holy Spirit.

ROMANS 8:28-30 - NOT EVERYTHING IS GOOD, BUT GOD CAN MAKE IT WORK FOR GOOD

28 And we know that God causes all things to work together for good to those who love God, to those who are called according to *His* purpose. **29** For those whom He foreknew, He also predestined *to become* conformed to the image of His Son, so that He would be the firstborn among many brethren; **30** and these whom He predestined, He also called; and these whom He called, He also justified; and these whom He justified, He also glorified.

Have you ever had a trial that made you ask, "Why is this happening to me?" Maybe you sighed, "What good can possibly come of this?" These Scriptures assure us that whenever trials and suffering come, God comes along with them and goes to work.

I once talked to a pastor who had the most horrible thing imaginable happen to his family. His two pre-teen sons were kidnapped and molested. One was violently beaten to death. The other child was beaten but survived. He was disfigured and partially blinded. As the father told me the story, I asked that same question. "Can anything good come from this evil thing that happened to his family?" He told me he asked the same question. Over the years the story went out in magazines and media and the message of forgiveness accompanied the horrible event. The family learned to rest in God and trust Him to do what God does best. The father then told me of a box he keeps in his office that contains hundreds upon hundreds of letters from people who came to Christ through their story. God caused the most evil thing to work for good.

Verses 28 and 30 are what some call the "Golden chain of redemption."

- **Foreknowledge**

- **Predestination**

- **Calling**

- **Justification**

- **Glorification**

We may never fully understand the depth of these doctrines on this side of glory. However, we do know one important thing, this is our story. We are known by God. We are selected and adopted into His forever family, called to do His work, pardoned from all our sins and raised to be seated with Christ in the heavenly places. That alone is enough to know that whatever comes our way, God will make it good for us because He loves us and wants the very best for us, even if that very best means we suffer for a season.

31 What then shall we say to these things? If God *is* for us, who *is* against us? **32** He who did not spare His own Son, but delivered Him over for us all, how will He not also with Him freely give us all things? **33** Who will bring a charge against God's elect? God is the one who justifies; **34** who is the one who condemns? Christ Jesus is He who died, yes, rather who was raised, who is at the right hand of God, who also intercedes for us. **35** Who will separate us from the love of Christ? Will tribulation, or distress, or persecution, or famine, or nakedness, or peril, or sword? **36** Just as it is written,

"For Your sake we are being put to death all day long;
We were considered as sheep to be slaughtered." *(Psalm 44:22)*

37 But in all these things we overwhelmingly conquer through Him who loved us. **38** For I am convinced that neither death, nor life, nor angels, nor principalities, nor things present, nor things to come, nor powers, **39** nor height, nor depth, nor any other created thing, will be able to separate us from the love of God, which is in Christ Jesus our Lord.

GOD IS FOR US

31 What then shall we say to these things? If God *is* for us, who *is* against us?

If there was ever one single sentence that removes all fear, it is this one. Everyone on earth can stand against us, threaten us, hate us, and do whatever else they want to do to us. In the end, the only thing that matters is what God says, not what people think (**verse 31**). We see that God is on our side, He is for us. That removes fear and doubt.

The passage goes on to give proof that God is on our side. He did not spare His Son **(verse 32).** He did that for us. The eternal God provided for our eternal life. He pardoned our sins and removed our guilt by placing it on His Son. The result is that no one can accuse us or lay any charge against us (**verses 33**). The risen Christ now sits at the right hand of God and acts as our intercessor and defense attorney (**verse 34**), always defending us against the enemy's accusations.

> "... if anyone sins, we have an Advocate with the Father, Jesus Christ the righteous;" (1 John 2:1)

ONE MORE TIME, CAN ANYTHING SEPARATE US FROM THE LOVE OF CHRIST? (ROMANS 8:35-39)

35 Who will separate us from the love of Christ? Will tribulation, or distress, or persecution, or famine, or nakedness, or peril, or sword?

*(The following is an abridged and summarized commentary of Charles Spurgeon on **Romans 8:35**)*

The apostle gives us a little summary of the evils that believers will face. This was common in the first-century persecutions of the Church.

Tribulation — The word "tribulation," in the Latin, signifies threshing (the beating of the grain to separate the wheat from the outer husks). God's people are often cast upon the threshing-floor to be beaten with the heavy strokes of trouble; but they are more than conquerors since they lose nothing but their straw and chaff, and the pure wheat is separated from that which was of no benefit to it. It is a similar concept of a hot

151

furnace and adequate time is used to melt precious metals and remove the impurities.

Distress — This describes a situation where we see no deliverance. Our mind is distracted in our mental storm, tossed here and there. A genuine Christian will come out of this all right. We are more than conquerors over mental distress.

Persecution — A good name has been slandered. False accusations, undeserved evil hurled against the child of God for no reason other than hatred for the cross of Christ. Instead of destroying the Church it has always strengthened her.

Famine — Not just mental distress or attack, but also extreme physical hardship. Pain and hunger.

Nakedness — We will always be clothed in the righteousness of Christ even if forced to walk in rags defending His name. Job responded to his unimaginable loss with the words, "Though He slay me, yet will I trust Him." We may suffer indignity while others look on, but only what God sees is what counts.

Peril — The apostle mentions next to nakedness, peril - that is, constant exposure to sudden death. It was the life of the early Christian. They were under continuous attack and threat from the Roman Empire. They could be banished or killed at any moment.

Sword—The final thing is the sword. Death is the final blow the world can make against the Christian. Jesus told His followers not to fear those who could kill the body but fear only God. History tells many stories of martyrs who sang on the way to the gallows or burning stake. "We are more than conquerors through Him that loved us." Paul supports this by quoting **Psalm 44** where the Psalmist describes living under the threat of death all day long.

WE HAVE THE ULTIMATE VICTORY AND HOPE

37 But in all these things we overwhelmingly conquer through Him who loved us. **38** For I am convinced that neither death, nor life, nor angels, nor principalities, nor things present, nor things to come, nor powers, **39** nor height, nor depth, nor any other created thing, will be able to separate us from the love of God, which is in Christ Jesus our Lord.

When does the Christian have victory? All the time. During times of tribulation, distress, persecution, famine, nakedness, peril, and threat of death. When we understand that these things do not conquer us, it is apparent that nothing will. The final three verses of **Romans 8** are one of the greatest passages God has given us to assure us that He will never leave us, and that we will never be cut off from Him.

The previous verses revealed that nothing we face, not even death itself will defeat us. No angel, good or bad (principalities) can alter our eternal hope in Christ. Nothing that exists today or that will come tomorrow or the next day will take us away from Jesus. No power on earth, or in the heavens, or from hell, can pull us from God's grip.

No created thing can separate us from Christ. That includes us since we are a created thing. The key to it all is to be "in Christ." There is no more secure place to be than "in Christ." The eternal hand of God, which grips us, is infinitely powerful. His grip on us is unbreakable.

As an old preacher once said, "If that doesn't light your fire, your wood is wet!"

PAUL ANSWERS ISRAEL'S COMPLAINTS

COMPLAINT

TO· **GOD**

WHOSE FAULT· **Yours** ☑

DESIRED OUTCOME· ☑ APOLOGY ☐ LITIGATION ☐ RESTITUTION ☐ EXPLANATION ☐ PROMOTION ☐ CHANGE

1. YOUR WORD HAS FAILED!
2. YOU ARE UNJUST!
3. WE CANNOT BE HELD RESPONSIBLE!

COMPLAINTANT _____ *ISRAEL*

OVERVIEW OF ROMANS 9

Israel had everything going for them. They were specifically chosen by God as the nation that would be the human channel for the Son of God. They were children of Abraham, Isaac, and Jacob. They were feared by the nations around them and custodians of the written Word of God. They were given the priests, the sacrifices, the feasts, the Temple, and the prophets. God traveled with them. God used mighty miracles to deliver His people from Egypt. He led them to a special land picked out just for them. They had it all. Yet many departed from the faith, some even going after pagan gods. At the same time, there were a small number who remained faithful to God. These are called the **Remnant**.

THE KEY VERSES FOR CHAPTER 9

[6] "But it is not as though the word of God has failed. For they are not all Israel who are descended from Israel; [7] nor are they all children because they are Abraham's descendants, but: "THROUGH ISAAC YOUR DESCENDANTS WILL BE NAMED." [8] That is, it is not the children of the flesh who are children of God, but the children of the promise are regarded as descendants."

SIMPLE OUTLINE

I. (9:1-3) Paul's great burden for His people.

II. (9:4, 5) Paul reminds Israel of all the privileges God had given them.

III. (9:6-8) When is an Israelite not an Israelite?

IV. (9:9-18) The indisputable sovereignty of God.

V. (9:19-22) A lesson from the potter's house.

VI. (9:23-32) The remnant of Israel and the mercy of God.

Romans Chapter 9

SOME PRELIMINARY MATTERS BEFORE WE BEGIN CHAPTER 9

Solving a 2,000-year-old puzzle?

There has been more controversy in the Christian church through-out history that has come from Romans chapter 9 than any other single chapter in the Bible.

Imagine if you were putting together a puzzle that only had four pieces. How hard would that be? But what if the puzzle was entitled "The Plan of God." The four puzzle pieces were God's Sovereignty, Man's Free Will, Predes-tination, and Personal Responsibility. In case you were wondering, the puzzle is still unsolved

and has been sitting on the table for 2,000 years. Maybe because only God has seen the picture on the box cover.

Listen to what two well-known Christians have said about this puzzle:

Charles Spurgeon (Calvinist)

> "That God predestines, and yet that man is responsible, are two facts that few can see clearly. They are believed to be inconsistent and contradictory, but they are not. The fault is in our weak judgment. Two truths cannot be contradictory to each other. If then, I find taught in one part of the Bible that everything is fore-ordained, that

is true; and I find that in another Scripture, that man is responsible for all his actions, that is true; and it is only my folly that leads me to imagine that these two truths can ever contradict each other. I do not believe they can ever be welded into one upon any earthly anvil, but they certainly shall be one in eternity."

Ravi Zacharias (non-Calvinist)

"I think you should view the sovereignty of God and the responsibility of man as a kind of a precious stone with two facets to it. When it catches the light from one direction, you see one color; when it catches the light from the other direction you see the other color. . . It is not possible for a finite person to infinitely understand the infinite. . . So my proposal to you is to see both of these perspectives and hold them in balance."

"Can you solve the mysteries of God?
Can you discover everything about the Almighty?"
(Job 11:7 New Living Translation (NLT)

"For as the heavens are higher than the earth, So are My ways higher than your ways and My thoughts than your thoughts." (Isaiah 55:9)

Chapter 9 plows directly into the most difficult theological fields and controversies found anywhere in the Bible. Paul confidently handles the complaints of his people by quoting numerous Old Testament passages that lift up God. There are some teachings that are so difficult that **Romans 9** has been referred to by some as the "Pastor's graveyard."

While it is good to be a lifetime student of God's Word, we each need a dose of humility when considering these immense matters. Do we think we can understand all the mysteries of God? Is it possible there are many things we don't yet see clearly? Is it not possible God has put together things we cannot?

Romans 9 Commentary

Paul's great burden for his people (9:1-3)

1 I am telling the truth in Christ, I am not lying, my conscience testifies with me in the Holy Spirit, **2** that I have great sorrow and unceasing grief in my heart. **3** For I could wish that I myself were accursed, *separated* from Christ for the sake of my brethren, my kinsmen according to the flesh,

Paul begins by reminding his listeners he is telling the truth. What he is about to tell them is so unbelievable that he felt he had to preface it with two things. First, that he is being absolutely truthful and even invokes the names of Christ and the Holy Spirit as his witness. He also tells them that what he says has been brought about by intense sorrow and grief. This sorrow is possibly because, as a former Pharisee, he had been a blind guide, leading his precious nation into the ditch of dead religion. Many of his countrymen had trusted him and he had been wrong. Paul felt guilt, sorrow, grief, and the compassion of Christ Himself. He cries out, ***"I could wish that I myself were accursed, separated from Christ for the sake of my brethren, my kinsmen according to the flesh,"***

If possible, Paul was willing to give up eternal life and spend eternity in Hell if only his people could be saved! Is there anyone in your life you would do that for? Think it through before you answer. It is what Jesus did when he became sin for us on the cross to pay our eternal penalty so we could become the righteousness of Christ in Him. **(2 Corinthians 5:21)**

Paul reminds Israel of all the privileges God had given them. (9:4, 5)

4 who are Israelites, to whom belongs the adoption as sons, and the glory and the covenants and the giving of the Law and the *temple* service and the promises, **5** whose are the fathers, and from whom is the Christ according to the flesh, who is over all, God blessed forever. Amen.

ISRAEL — GOD'S SPECIAL, CHOSEN PEOPLE

No other people were given so much. Paul lists the privileges they enjoyed.

Israelites (Verse 4) — When the Israelites left Egypt, God traveled with them. The miracles and exploits of Israel became known everywhere they went. Their very name terrorized the nations. In the words of Rahab, their God was the God of Heaven and earth.

> **"I know that the Lord has given you the land, and that the terror of you has fallen on us, and that all the inhabitants of the land have melted away before you. 10 For we have heard how the Lord dried up the water of the Red Sea before you when you came out of Egypt, and what you did to the two kings of the Amorites who were beyond the Jordan, to Sihon and Og, whom you utterly destroyed. 11 When we heard it, our hearts melted and no courage remained in any man any longer because of you; for the Lord your God, He is God in heaven above and on earth beneath.** (Joshua 2:8-12)

What a privilege to be an Israelite, the people of the great God.

Adopted as Sons into the Family of God (Verse 4) — The only way a person can be in God's family is to be adopted. To be adopted also means that they are chosen, handpicked by the Father to be a part of the family of God. That is why Ruth said to Naomi, *"for where you go, I will go, and where you lodge, I will lodge. Your people shall be my people, and your God, my God."* **(Ruth 1:16)**. Many in Israel had lost sight of that immense privilege.

The Glory of God (Verse 4) — Every nation in the region knew God traveled with Israel across the desert and into Canaan and into Jerusalem. The glory of God filled the Tabernacle and then later, the Temple. A pillar of fire at night, a cloud and canopy by day. Even Moses' face glowed from being in the presence of God. Israel did not have a god of stone or wood, they worshiped the God of Glory.

The Covenants (Verse 4) — God established, with Israel alone, two unique Covenants. He promised He would one day bless all nations through them. That was the Abrahamic Covenant. The Messiah, Jesus, fulfilled this redemptive promise when He died and rose again.

The second covenant was the Davidic Covenant. God promised David that one day a great King would come from his family line. Jesus will fulfill that promise at this second coming when Satan is removed as the prince of this world, and the rightful King takes His throne. Jesus came the first time for His people, and He is coming again for His Kingdom. What an amazing heritage to have as an Israelite.

The Law of God (Verse 4) — God's people were given His Law. They had His moral guidelines in the Ten Commandments, so they knew how to live with both God and their neighbor. They also had the ceremonial law which gave them a way back to

God. God's Law made them a unique, civilized, and prosperous people. Most importantly, it was God's way of exposing their sin and driving them to repentance and eternal life.

The Temple (Verse 4) —Every heathen nation worshiped something. They had their high places and elaborate temples for their false gods. The Israelites had the true God, and the system God had set up to show all men that they have sinned. God had one way back to Himself, through faith. God was a God of love and grace, so different from the false gods of the heathen who demanded children be thrown into the fire.

The Promises (Verse 4) — God promised that they would be His people. God promised that one day they would bring in His Messiah, the greatest promise of all. God promised His presence and protection, if they would only believe and follow Him. God sent great prophets to bring messages of warning and hope to remind them of His promises. They were a people of the promises of God.

The Heritage of the Fathers (Verse 5) — They were of the lineage of Abraham, Isaac, and Jacob. Jacob was given the new name Israel. His twelve sons were to become the tribes of the people of God, the family line of promise. There was no greater family line.

The Messiah, Christ, God become Flesh (Verse 5) — That family line, that heritage leads all the way to the fulfillment of what the prophets foretold.

> **"But as for you, Bethlehem Ephrathah,**
> **Too little to be among the clans of Judah,**
> **From you One will go forth for Me to be ruler in Israel.**
> **His goings forth are from long ago,**
> **From the days of eternity."** (Micah 5:2)

No other people on earth had such privileges.

161

Romans 9:5 makes it clear that Jesus is the One from eternity past that has come. He **"is the Christ according to the flesh, who is over all, God blessed forever. Amen."** This is one of the strong statements in Scripture confirming the Deity of Jesus Christ. Two of the greatest Greek scholars, Wuest and Robertson, agree that this passage can only mean Christ is Himself, God.

Of all the privileges Israel had, there was none greater than to be the chosen people of the Messiah. Jesus was born of the Jews. He is the King of the Jews.

Paul, in **verses 1-3** had just poured out his heart and described his grief for his people, and now in **verses 4 and 5** he reminds Israel just how special they are. God has used them in history to bring salvation to the nations. For us today, it is a similar reminder of all God has done for us. It is our responsibility to bring that message to the lost.

When is an Israelite not an Israelite? (9:6-8)

Israel had so much. But with such privilege, comes great responsibility. Unfortunately, history reveals that a large portion of God's chosen children squandered their great privileges. Jesus referred to that in the parable of the prodigal son in **Luke 15.** It is the story of two brothers and a faithful and loving father. One brother wastes his inheritance, even bringing shame to his family. However, he repents and is restored to the family as a son. So it was with Israe. Some repented and by faith became true Israel, "children of promise." Some trusted in their physical family line, children of Abraham, and depended on that birthright to save them. They are called "children of the flesh," **(Verse 8)**

This passage will introduce two Israels. One claimed they were God's people, because of who their earthly father was. The other because of their faith in God. One of them became part of the family of God, but the other is still standing outside of the feast looking in and refusing to enter.

Now, let's look at **verses 6-8**.

BIRTHRIGHT OR THE RIGHT BIRTH? (ROMANS 9:6-8)

6 But *it is* **not as though the word of God has failed**. For they are not all Israel who are *descended* from Israel; **7** nor are they all children because they are Abraham's descendants, but: "**THROUGH ISAAC YOUR DESCENDANTS WILL BE NAMED.**" *(Genesis 21:12)* **8** That is, it is not the children of the flesh who are children of God, but the children of the promise are regarded as descendants.

In a previous chapter, we looked at the Gospel of John where there is a description of what it takes to be a believer in Christ.

> [12] "But as many as received Him, to them He gave the right to become children of God, *even* to those who believe in His name, [13] who were born, not of blood nor of the will of the flesh nor of the will of man, but of God." (John 1:12, 13)

We learn from this text that there are several ways people thought they could be right with God, but they don't work. The true way is to receive Christ by believing in His name. Faith is the only way a person comes to God. When he does that, John says we are "born of God."

John lists three births that will <u>not lead to salvation</u>. They are:

- **Born of blood**. Trusting in a family line. A person might say, "I am from the line of Abraham. It is my birthright."

John says, "not of blood." No birthright can save a person.

- **Born of the will of the flesh.** Trusting in our good works will not save us. Salvation is a work of God's Spirit not a work of human flesh or effort.

- **Born of the will of man.** Trusting in someone else. Some claim to be God's people because they were baptized or circumcised as a child. Salvation is not based on what someone else does for us or to us.

Paul is making these same comparisons in **Romans 9:6-8**. He does this by comparing being a child of Abraham to being a child of Isaac. Aren't these the same? Not necessarily.

Abraham was declared righteous by God because of his faith. He was saved by faith. He had two sons, Ishmael and Isaac. Ishmael was not the chosen son, not the child of the promise. Abraham initially tried to fulfill God's promises opn his own. That resulted in Ishmael. Isaac was the miracle child. The son God promised in Abraham's old age. Both had Abraham as their father. However, only Isaac is called the child of the promises of God.

Isaac had two sons as well. Jacob was the chosen one. He would later be named Israel. Esau, in despising his birthright, was rejected by God. Paul uses this lineage to describe two types of people, children of the flesh and children of the promise. True children of Israel are referred to as descendants of Isaac.

This is a very important distinction. Children of the flesh vs. children of the promise. **Not everyone who claimed to be Israel was true Israel in God's eye.**

ISRAEL'S THREE COMPLAINTS AGAINST GOD

Chapter 9 identifies and addresses three major complaints that Israel had against God. **Verse 6** reveals the first one. **They felt that God's Word had failed them.** What happened to the blessings God had promised? Why had they endured Egyptian bondage and Babylonian captivity, the destruction of the Temple and other judgments? Why had God been silent for 400 years when they needed God their King to come and rescue them from slavery from the nations? They complained that the Word of God had failed.

Their second objection is found in **verse 14**. **They blamed God as being unjust.** The third objection is found in **verse 19**. **They believed they were not responsible for their actions** because God made them the way they were. They were like His puppets. They could only do what He made them do.

Today, whenever the doctrine of election is discussed, the last two objections are still the most common complaints. God is unjust, He picks some and not others. Therefore, I am not responsible since God did it all. In other words, God is to blame. He created and runs everything. He is responsible for the sin in the world. Therefore, He is ultimately responsible for my sin.

Their complaints come from a wrong understanding of God's justice and mercy. God is being accused of being unjust.

Think about it. All people are born sinners and separated from God. If God acted justly, then everyone would go into hell. This is about mercy to the one who deserves punishment. God is never unjust when He punishes sin. It is because of the mercy of God that anyone is rescued. It is all undeserved. Through all of it, God remains just.

What is lacking in each of these three complaints against God is faith. Israel began trusting in their heritage and not leaning on faith in God. Many in Israel called themseves children of Abraham, but not of the line of faith.

> **"Paul tells us that no one is truly Israel unless he is governed by God. We have a parallel situation with the word 'Christian.' Not everyone who is called a Christian is truly a follower of Christ."** (Chuck Smith)

This next section of **Romans 9** will bring us back to those four puzzle pieces.

The Indisputable Sovereignty of God. (9:9-18)

Remember those four puzzle pieces that I said no one has ever been able to adequately put together? They are the sovereignty of God, the free will of man, predestination, and the responsibility of man. These four things are all taught in Scripture. Differing views often have differing definitions.

The primary attribute of God that is the central focus of this next section, **Romans 9:9-18** is God's Sovereignty.

Let's begin with some simple definitions.

SOVEREIGNTY OF GOD:

Sovereignty is the right of God to do as He wishes **(Psalm 50:1, Isaiah 40:15, 1 Timothy 6:15)** with His creation. He is rightfully free to do everything according to His will.

The Westminster Confession of Faith says,'

> **"God, from all eternity, did, by the wisest and holy counsel of His own will, freely, and unchangeably, ordain whatever comes to pass."**

FREE WILL OF MAN:

Free will is the freedom of self-determination and action independent of external causes. It is the ability to make choices. Free will is generally viewed two ways:

- **Determinism** — Man's free will is damaged severely by the fall and restricted by his sinful nature. He is incapable of choosing God. **(1 Cor. 2:14, Rom. 3:10-12, Rom. 6:14-20)**. (Calvinism)

- **Libertarianism** — Man is not enslaved by sin so that he can only choose sinful things. He can freely choose to accept or reject God in spite of his sinful nature **(John 3:16, 3:36)**. (Non-Calvinism)

AW Tozer summarized the big questions many ask when he wrote:

> **"ANOTHER real problem created by the doctrine of the divine sovereignty has to do with the will of man. If God rules His universe by His sovereign decrees, how is it possible for a man to exercise free choice? And if he cannot exercise freedom of choice, how can he be held responsible for his conduct? Is he not a mere puppet whose actions are determined by a behind-the-scenes God who pulls the strings as it pleases Him?"**

PREDESTINATION:

Predestination/Election refers to the sovereign act of God choosing nations and/or individuals to carry out His purpose in the world. Election is based solely on the sovereignty of God.

RESPONSIBILITY OF MAN:

God has entrusted humankind, both individually and collectively, with free choice and responsibility. Humankind is, therefore, answerable to God. Our sin-nature seeks to deny responsibility

167

and blame others or God for our failures.

Now, since **Romans 9** focuses strongly on the sovereignty of God, we will look at that a bit more in depth.

Everyone believes in the sovereignty of God

The differences today in theological systems is how sovereignty is viewed. Just about everyone claims to believe in it. Think of a king over a country, called a sovereign ruler. He has the right to dictate every law, orchestrate every event and demand allegiance. He punishes those who oppose him. He could sovereignly choose to give individuals freedom and rights of self-government under His authority. That is also a sovereign decision. God could write the entire script of humanity, or He could direct a play that allowed the actors freedom of individual expression. In either case, God is sovereignly choosing which way it works for His Glory.

Doing something or doing nothing can both be exercises of God's sovereignty.

> **"Jesus taught his disciples to pray 'Thy will be done, on earth as it is in heaven' (Mt 6:10 RSV). If God's sovereignty were already completely exercised, why would anyone need to pray for God's will to be done on earth? In that case, it would always already be done on earth."** (Olson)

Example – God is the Sovereign over the entire universe. Satan is called the prince and power of the air, the world where we live. The entire world comes under his grasp. How can both God and Satan be in control?

God is the Sovereign over all. In His sovereign decision He has given the enemy a season of free reign (but still under God's boundaries and time line). Satan is a prince, but God is King. For now, on earth, God is sovereign by nature, right and power and will one day be seen as He is, the Sovereign over all (**1 Corinthians 15:28**) at the completion of time. God will be sovereign in the fully accomplished role He has always possessed. It is in some ways like Jesus, who for a season, set aside certain divine privileges to accomplish our salvation. In the end, God is God, the Sovereign. All His decisions are sovereign, even the times when He allows others to determine their own direction. That is His sovereign decision.

Somehow in the infinite wisdom and knowledge of God, He has combined what man cannot. He put the puzzle together.

Now let's look at one of the most troubling passages found in the Bible, Romans 8:9-18

JACOB AND ESAU

9 For this is the word of promise: **"AT THIS TIME I WILL COME, AND SARAH SHALL HAVE A SON."** *(Genesis 18:14)* **10** And not only this, but there was Rebekah also, when she had conceived *twins* by one man, our father Isaac; **11** for though *the twins* were not yet born and had not done anything good or bad, so that God's purpose according to *His* choice would stand, not because of works but because of Him who calls, **12** it was said to her, **"THE OLDER WILL SERVE THE YOUNGER."** **13** Just as it is written, **"JACOB I LOVED, BUT ESAU I HATED."**

A similar Old Testament Scripture is **Malachi 1:2, 3**

> [2] "I have loved you," says the Lord. But you say, "How have You loved us?" "Was not Esau Jacob's brother?" declares the Lord. "Yet I have loved Jacob; [3] but I have hated Esau, and I have made his mountains a desolation and appointed his inheritance for the jackals of the wilderness."

(Malachi 1:2, 3)

Jacob and Esau

God promised Abraham a son. That son, the son of the promise, was Isaac. Isaac had two sons, but God chose the younger, Jacob, to continue the line of the promises given to Abraham and Isaac. The elder son, Esau, angered God. The line of Esau would become enemies of God. Amalek, the grandson of Esau, would become the worst of God's enemies, the Amalekites. God proclaimed judgment and annihilation against the Amalekites, the line of Esau:

> [17] **"Remember what Amalek did to you along the way when you came out from Egypt, [18] how he met you along the way and attacked among you all the stragglers at your rear when you were faint and weary; and he did not fear God. [19] Therefore it shall come about when the Lord your God has given you rest from all your surrounding enemies, in the land which the Lord your God gives you as an inheritance to possess, you shall blot out the memory of Amalek from under heaven; you must not forget."**
>
> (DEUTERONOMY 25:17-19)

Romans 9 describes the love God had for Jacob, and the hatred He had for Esau, the son who despised his birthright.

DID GOD CHOOSE JACOB TO BE SAVED AND ESAU TO BE LOST BEFORE HE WAS BORN?

This passage and that question may be the most controversial thought found anywhere in Scripture.

Recent surveys of the Evangelical church in North America show that the church is split almost equally between those who say "Yes" and those who say "No."

How is it possible for Christians to have such different views on Biblical topics?

The answer to that question lies in our inability to fully understand God. We will not fully agree on how sovereignty and election can work with a free will and personal responsibility. Both, as we have seen, are found in Scripture, and both are true. Once again, it is a puzzle we can't put together. However, in the knowledge and wisdom of God, He has done it.

As might be expected, many have tried to come up with solutions to this passage which allow for both the sovereignty of God and the free will of man.

SOLUTION ONE – GOD LIVES IN THE ETERNAL PRESENT

To God all of eternal past, present and future are now.

Jesus once told the Pharisees, "Before Abraham was, I am." These are the same words God told Moses when Moses asked God His name, He said, "I am!" God does not have a past, present or future. He always is. Ten thousand years from now in our time system and the way we think, God is. He is just as aware of what is happening ten thousand years from now as He is the things that are happening in the present or in the past. All

171

of eternity is "now" to God. He created space, time, and matter and is outside of all of it. We refer to this as **God's eternality.** When God said He hated Esau before he was born, God already knew the entire story of Esau before he was born. When you consider God's eternality along with His Omniscience, one must conclude that God always is and always knows it all. If He didn't, He wouldn't be God. We can't begin to understand the depths of just these two attributes of God, yet there is much more.

In the case of God loving Jacob and hating Esau before the children were actually born, it makes sense that the eternally present God has always seen and known all of eternity past, present and future. He fully knew all the choices of Esau, the children of Esau, the Amalekites (Amalek was Esau's grandson), their hatred for Israel and plans to destroy Israel throughout time. Before Jacob and Esau were born, God already knew the entire story and loved Jacob and hated Esau. Esau was the one who despised God by selling his birthright, the right to be the one to father the continuing family line that would one day bring in the Messiah, Jesus Christ. But Esau sold that privilege for a bowl of soup. God in His infinite omniscience and eternal presence knew all that before Esau was actually born.

To be fair, there are other views of this passage.

SOLUTION TWO – HATE CAN MEAN "LOVES LESS."

There are places in the Bible where "hate" seems to mean something like **"loved less" (Genesis 29:31, 33; Deuteronomy 21:15; Matthew 6:24; Luke 14:26; John 12:25).**

> **"If anyone comes to Me and does not hate his own father and mother and wife and children and brothers and sisters, yes, and even his own life, he cannot be My disciple."**
> (Luke 14:26)

SOLUTION THREE – THE WORDS "JACOB" AND "ESAU" REFER TO THE NATIONS THEY BIRTHED, NOT THE INDIVIDUALS.

In **Genesis 25:23** the Lord told Rebekah *"Two nations are in thy womb, and two manner of people shall be separated from thy bowels; and the one people shall be stronger than the other people; and the elder shall serve the younger."*

Election/Predestination is generally viewed in two ways:

- **Election to Salvation.** God chooses who will be saved or lost. This is referred to as Unconditional Election and Irresistible Calling. God decides everything, even the eternal destiny of each person. He picked Jacob to be saved and Esau to be lost. (Calvinism)

- **Election to Service.** God chose the nation that would come from Jacob rather than the nation from Esau to fulfill His overall strategy in history. God had a great historical purpose to send His Son into the world to pay the penalty of sin for all people and nations. (Non-Calvinism). The choosing of the nation Israel was to bless all people, Jew and Gentile.

The ultimate decisions are from God. He alone is sovereign, always just, righteous and merciful. He is eternally present through all time. Many in Israel had come to believe that God was unjust. He picked winners and losers. That was not fair.

This is the issue Paul answers in the next three verses.

14 What shall we say then? There is no injustice with God, is there? May it never be! **15** For He says to Moses, **"I WILL HAVE MERCY ON WHOM I HAVE MERCY, AND I WILL HAVE COMPASSION ON WHOM I HAVE COMPASSION."** *(Exodus 33:19)* **16** So then **it _does_ not _depend_ on the man** who wills or the man who runs **but on God who has mercy**.

Is everything preordained, or does man have some influence on his eternal destiny? The answer appears to be "Yes!" Yes to both. Both are taught in the Bible.

There are clear passages in the Bible that God is in complete control and even predestines. There are also clear passages that show that man is judged based on his choices and life decisions. Man is told he needs to choose who he will serve and we are told we are chosen. These are puzzle pieces we cannot put together and that is OK. I find comfort that God is much bigger than we are. He has it all worked out.

Let's look at mercy for a moment, since it is mentioned three times in these three verses. The compassion of God is mentioned twice.

> **"Mercy is not getting what we deserve (punishment). God is never less than fair with anyone but fully reserves the right to be more than fair with individuals as He chooses."**
> (Blue Letter Commentary)

Example: Suppose two men are on death row for murder and awaiting execution. They are both guilty. **Does the sovereign ruler of the land have the legal right to pardon the guilty and set them free?** Yes. Does He have the right to pardon one of the two? Yes. If He pardons only one of the two, does the one who must still be executed have a right to say that the sovereign isn't fair?

Jesus told a parable that gives us insight into this question.

THE LABORERS IN THE VINEYARD (MATTHEW 20:1-16)

> **"For the kingdom of heaven is like a landowner who went out early in the morning to hire laborers for his vineyard.
> ² When he had agreed with the laborers for a denarius for the day, he sent them into his vineyard. ³ And he went out about the third hour and saw others standing idle in the**

market place; ⁴ and to those he said, 'You also go into the vineyard, and whatever is right I will give you.' And so they went. ⁵ Again he went out about the sixth and the ninth hour, and did the same thing. ⁶ And about the eleventh hour he went out and found others standing around; and he *said to them, 'Why have you been standing here idle all day long?' ⁷ They said to him, 'Because no one hired us.' He said to them, 'You go into the vineyard too.'

⁸ "When evening came, the owner of the vineyard said to his foreman, 'Call the laborers and pay them their wages, beginning with the last group to the first.' ⁹ When those hired about the eleventh hour came, each one received a denarius. ¹⁰ When those hired first came, they thought that they would receive more; but each of them also received a denarius. ¹¹ When they received it, they grumbled at the landowner, ¹² saying, 'These last men have worked only one hour, and you have made them equal to us who have borne the burden and the scorching heat of the day.' ¹³ But he answered and said to one of them, 'Friend, I am doing you no wrong; did you not agree with me for a denarius? ¹⁴ Take what is yours and go, but I wish to give to this last man the same as to you. ¹⁵ Is it not lawful for me to do what I wish with what is my own? Or is your eye envious because I am generous?' ¹⁶ So the last shall be first, and the first last."

Since all are born dead in sin and deserving the wrath of God **(Ephesians 2:1-3)**, God is not required to pardon anyone. If God chooses to pardon a lost undeserving sinner, then the lost undeserving sinner who doesn't get pardoned has no just complaint against God.

All are lost and destined for perdition. God does not have to choose them for hell. They are already headed there because of their inherent and imputed sin, and the sins they commit. God is never unjust.

"I WILL HAVE MERCY ON WHOM I HAVE MERCY"
(Romans 9:15)

THE HARDENING OF PHARAOH'S HEART (9:17, 18)

17 For the Scripture says to Pharaoh, **"FOR THIS VERY PURPOSE I RAISED YOU UP, TO DEMONSTRATE MY POWER IN YOU, AND THAT MY NAME MIGHT BE PROCLAIMED THROUGHOUT THE WHOLE EARTH."** *(Exodus 9:16)* **18** So then He has mercy on whom He desires, and He hardens whom He desires.

The story of Pharaoh is an interesting study. **Verses 17 and 18** state that God is the one who raised up Pharaoh in order to demonstrate His power and show forth His Glory. God hardened Pharaoh's heart to accomplish this.

Exodus also says this very thing.

> **"Then the LORD said to Moses, "Go to Pharaoh, for I have hardened his heart and the heart of his servants, that I may perform these signs of Mine among them,"**
> (Exodus 10:1)

Exodus also is clear in several places that Pharaoh hardened his own heart.

> **"But Pharaoh hardened his heart this time also, and he did not let the people go."** (Exodus 8:32)

Other verses in that same section of Exodus tell us simply that Pharaoh's heart was hardened without saying who caused it or how it happened.

> **"Pharaoh's heart was hardened, and he did not let the sons of Israel go, just as the LORD had spoken through Moses."** (Exodus 9:35)

How can both Pharaoh harden his heart and God harden Pharaoh's heart? One theologian explained it this way, **The same sun that melts wax hardens clay.** If a person's heart is receptive to God, it will melt. If it is stubborn and rebellious, God will only harden it further.

Maybe we can't fully understand how it all works, but we do know God used Pharaoh to demonstrate His power to His people and bring glory to His name.

> **"To Moses, God exercised mercy, and toward Pharaoh God exercised His justice. God was just in both cases, and interestingly, God used both men to further His purposes. God raised up Moses to be a deliverer of His people and a type of Messiah to come. God raised up Pharaoh to display His great power and to proclaim His glory: "For the Scripture says to Pharaoh, 'For this very purpose I raised you up, to demonstrate My power in you, and that my name might be proclaimed throughout the whole earth"**
> (Bible.org)

It was the hardening of Pharaoh's heart that brought about the freedom of the Hebrew children from 400 years of bondage. God used the hardening, or partial blindness, of Israel to bring in many from the Gentile nations. His grace flows from His sovereign justice.

The overall message to Israel in the first part of **Romans 9** is that God truly loves Israel. They were given a very privileged assignment, position, and purpose in the plan of God to redeem lost humanity and bring glory to Himself. Many confused that privilege as something they deserved. Their privilege became pride. God is bringing them back to the basic truth that it wasn't them at all, but God who deserves all the glory. He reminds Israel that they are just a lump of clay, no different from the other nations. What made them different was the sovereign choice of God, not something they did or deserved. It is God that raises up nations and peoples to accomplish His perfect will.

Next section: God takes us to the potter's house.

A lesson from the potter's house (Romans 9:19-22)

19 You will say to me then, "Why does He still find fault? For who resists His will?" **20** On the contrary, who are you, O man, <u>who answers back to God?</u> The thing molded will not say to the molder, "<u>Why did you make me like this,</u>" will it? **21** Or does not the potter have a right over the clay, to make from the **same lump** one vessel for <u>**honorable use**</u> and another for <u>**common use?**</u> **22**What if God, although willing to demonstrate His wrath and to make His power known, endured with much patience vessels of wrath prepared for destruction?

God waited patiently while those who rejected Him and put themselves on a path to destruction ran out their course.

Does God make us either a vessel of glory or a vessel of wrath? Is our only role to play out our part like clay in a potter's hand? Is, as Shakespeare said, "All the world's a stage, and all the men and women merely players."?

Do we have any responsibility if the decisions are all God's?

One thing to note:
"I am fascinated by Paul's reference to the fact that both vessels of mercy and vessels of wrath are made from the same lump. The same lump (Romans 9:21) is not the lump of innocent and deserving individuals, but the same barrel of rotten apples. Each of us deserves the wrath of God."

(Bible.org)

The image of the potter and clay was well known to Israel.

> "This is the word that came to Jeremiah from the Lord:
> "Go down to the potter's house, and there I will give you
> my message." So I went down to the potter's house, and I
> saw him working at the wheel. But the pot he was shap-
> ing from the clay was marred in his hands; so the potter
> formed it into another pot, shaping it as seemed best to
> him. Then the word of the Lord came to me. He said, "Can
> I not do with you, Israel, as this potter does?" declares
> the Lord. "Like clay in the hand of the potter, so are you in
> my hand, Israel. If at any time I announce that a nation or
> kingdom is to be uprooted, torn down and destroyed, and
> if that nation I warned repents of its evil, then I will relent
> and not inflict on it the disaster I had planned. And if at
> another time I announce that a nation or kingdom is to
> be built up and planted, and if it does evil in my sight and
> does not obey me, then I will reconsider the good I had
> intended to do for it."
> *(*Jeremiah 18:1-10**)**

Is the hardening of Israel His decree (Calvinism), or His response (Arminianism) to their unbelief?

> "When Paul says that there are vessels of wrath prepared
> (fitted) for destruction, we should not think that God has
> prepared them so. Those vessels do an adequate job on
> their own." (Blue Letter Bible commentary)

All vessels of wrath have fitted themselves for destruction. That
is why they can never blame God and say that He made them
that way.

Matthew 22 shows us that the lost will have only themselves
to blame. The king in the parable invites many to the wedding
feast, but one shows up without proper wedding clothes.

> [11] "But when the king came in to look over the dinner
> guests, he saw a man there who was not dressed in wed-
> ding clothes, [12] and he *said to him, 'Friend, how did you
> come in here without wedding clothes?' And the man was

speechless. ¹³ Then the king said to the servants, 'Bind him hand and foot, and throw him into the outer darkness; in that place there will be weeping and gnashing of teeth.' ¹⁴ For many are called, but few are chosen."

(Matthew 22:1-14)

The improperly dressed man had only himself to blame for his actions. That is why he was speechless. He stood condemned. He had the same opportunities as the others to dress properly.

If God made people like robots and programmed them to do certain things and play out a script already written, then they would say they had no option but to do what they had to do. The very serious problem for those who say the sovereignty of God means everything is prescripted, or written in advance, is that there is no real free will, and God is the author of evil.

19 You will say to me then, "Why does He still find fault? For who resists His will?"

The word "resist" from Wuest's Greek word studies:

> "(19-20) "to set one's self against, to withstand, resist, oppose." The man who resists God is one who defiantly rejects the God of the Bible. A face to face confrontation. His anger and defiance challenge the will and holiness of the One who created him. This is not a person who simply does not understand or chooses to believe other things.
>
> "The question means who can resist Him? Paul leaves the question unanswered, for there is no answer which a finite mind can either reason out nor understand since it involves the sovereignty of God and the fact of man as a free moral agent. The point where both of these touch each other has never been found by man." (Wuest's word studies from the Greek New Testament: for the English reader)

The last question posed in **verse 22** was "What if God, although willing to demonstrate His wrath and to make His power known, endured with much patience vessels of wrath prepared for destruction?)" The final section of **Romans 9** (and chapters 10 and 11) reveal God's purposes in His sovereign dealings. He is ultimately raising up a people from Israel (the Remnant) and the Gentiles to bring glory to Himself.

The Remnant of Israel and the mercy of God (Romans 9:23-32)

23 And *He did so* to make known the riches of His glory upon vessels of mercy, which He prepared beforehand for glory, **24** *even* us, whom He also called, not from among Jews only, but also from among Gentiles. **25** As He says also in Hosea,

"**I WILL CALL THOSE WHO WERE NOT MY PEOPLE, 'MY PEOPLE,'**
AND HER WHO WAS NOT BELOVED, 'BELOVED.'" *(Hosea 2:1)*
for the word beloved, one who receives compassion)
26 "**AND IT SHALL BE THAT IN THE PLACE WHERE IT WAS SAID TO THEM, 'YOU ARE NOT MY PEOPLE,'** *(Hosea 2:23)*
THERE THEY SHALL BE CALLED SONS OF THE LIVING GOD."
(Hosea 1:10)

Paul quotes several passages from the Hosea to show that God would raise up a believing remnant from His people, Israel.

> "You are not My people": These passages show how merciful God is. God told the prophet Hosea to name one of his children Lo-Ammi, meaning "Not My People." Yet God also promised that this judgment would not last forever. One day Israel would be restored and once again be called sons of the living God." (Blue Letter Bible Commentary)

Why would Paul quote specifically from Hosea?

"Hosea was the prophet who was to marry a harlot. His relationship with his adulterous wife was a picture of Israel's infidelity to God. Because of the infidelity of Israel, God disowned them, so that they were no longer His people. But God also promised that after their chastening He would once again draw them to Himself and call them His people." (Bible.org)

27 Isaiah cries out concerning Israel, "**THOUGH THE NUMBER OF THE SONS OF ISRAEL BE LIKE THE SAND OF THE SEA, IT IS THE <u>REMNANT</u> THAT WILL BE SAVED; 28 FOR THE LORD WILL EXECUTE HIS WORD ON THE EARTH, THOROUGHLY AND QUICKLY.**" *(Isaiah 10:22, 23)* **29** And just as Isaiah foretold,

"**UNLESS THE LORD OF <u>SABAOTH</u>** *(HOSTS, HEAVENLY ARMY, the LORD of Heaven's Armies NLT)* **HAD LEFT TO US A POSTERITY, WE WOULD HAVE BECOME LIKE SODOM, AND WOULD HAVE RESEMBLED GOMORRAH.**" *(Isaiah 1:9)*

The Remnant that will be saved will be true believers from the nation of Israel who have remained faithful to God. These are true Israel. They are the ones referred to in **Romans 11** when Paul looks forward to the great day when "All Israel will be saved," when the final roll call is complete, along with all the believing Gentiles. It may be only a remnant that survives, but at least there is a remnant!

By quoting many supporting Old Testament passages, Paul shows that nothing frustrates the will of God, even Israel's unbelief. It was all predicted and will be fulfilled. God even uses Israel's unbelief to bless the Gentile world. The conclusion of all of this is faith. It was always about faith. Without faith, we cannot please God.

30 What shall we say then? That Gentiles, who did not pursue righteousness, attained righteousness, even the righteousness which is by faith; **31** but Israel, pursuing a law of righteousness, did not arrive at *that* law. **32** Why? Because *they did* not *pursue it* by faith, but as though *it were* by works. They stumbled over the stumbling stone, **33** just as it is written,

"BEHOLD, I LAY IN ZION A STONE OF STUMBLING AND A ROCK OF OFFENSE,
AND HE WHO BELIEVES IN HIM WILL NOT BE DISAPPOINTED."
(Isaiah 28:16)

Verse 32 tells us that the lost are those who did not pursue faith but chose works whether it be Jew or Gentile.

Is the lost man lost because God made him a vessel of wrath, or because the man himself chose the wrong path? Remember the puzzle at the beginning? Just because we don't fully understand the sovereignty and wisdom of our infinite Creator and Savior, does not mean that God is unjust. His Word has never failed. We are responsible for our actions. That is a clear lesson from this chapter.

Some ask how a God of love can send anyone to hell. The better question is how can a Holy and Righteous God accept anyone into Heaven? The answer is Jesus.

We should not leave this chapter without a spirit of wonder and adoration. We dare not focus on the question, "Why not others?" We should exclaim "Why me!" The wonder of it all is that God chose us.

SO MUCH TO BE THANKFUL FOR

In this chapter the character of God and our proper attitude toward His Sovereignty are at stake. He is the potter and we are the clay.

When Jesus stood at the grave of Lazarus, His friend, He called out, "Lazarus, come forth!" He could have just said "Come forth!" What would have happened? Every tomb would have opened. He is the resurrection and the life. Only Lazarus came forth, and it brought glory to God. Do you think God was unfair that only Lazarus was called? We who believe have been called from the dead and raised and seated with Christ. I may not fully understand how it all works but I am so thankful for our God, the One who alone knows the solution to the puzzle.

WHO ARE YOU, O MAN, WHO ANSWERS BACK TO GOD? THE THING MOLDED WILL NOT SAY TO THE MOLDER, "WHY DID YOU MAKE ME LIKE THIS," WILL IT? 21 OR DOES NOT THE POTTER HAVE A RIGHT OVER THE CLAY?

(Romans 9:20, 21)

Romans Chapter 10

"For Christ is the end of the law for righteousness to everyone who believes."
(Romans 10:4)

CHAPTER OVERVIEW

Chapter 9 showcased the incomparable sovereignty of God. Paul showed that the three big objections the Jews raised were based on a poor understanding of God and His Word. They felt the Word had failed, God was not just and finally, they were not responsible for their failings. Paul refuted these complaints against God and defended the sovereignty of God.

In **Chapter 10,** Paul continues by showing Israel that their righteousness is really self-righteousness, because it is based on human works instead of true faith in God. Israel is responsible for their turning from the path of true faith and cannot blame God. **Chapter 9** focused on the sovereignty of God. Now **Chapter 10** puts the spotlight on the choices of man and human responsibility.

THE KEY VERSES FOR CHAPTER 10

[11] **"For the Scripture says, "WHOEVER BELIEVES IN HIM WILL NOT BE DISAPPOINTED." [12] For there is no distinction between Jew and Greek; for the same Lord is Lord of all, abounding in riches for all who call on Him; [13] for "WHOEVER WILL CALL ON THE NAME OF THE LORD WILL BE SAVED."**

SIMPLE OUTLINE

I. Romans 10:1-4. Israel chose to establish their own righteousness apart from God.

II. Romans 10:5-13. True righteousness comes by faith in God, not by man's works.

III. Romans 10:14-15. The Gospel must be preached.

IV. Romans 10:16-21. Many in Israel rejected the Gospel.

Romans 10 Commentary

Israel chose to establish their own righteousness apart from God (1-4)

1 Brethren, my heart's desire and my prayer to God for them is for *their* salvation.

Paul begins this chapter the same way he began **Chapter Nine**. He loved his people Israel. His greatest heart's desire was for them to come to the knowledge of the truth and trust Christ alone for their salvation, just as he had done.

2 For I testify about them that they have a zeal for God, but not in accordance with knowledge. **3** For not knowing about God's righteousness and seeking to establish their own, they did not subject themselves to the righteousness of God. **4** For Christ is the end of the law for righteousness to everyone who believes.

For the nation of Israel to come to true faith, they had to set aside one huge obstacle, themselves and their self-righteous path of trying to save themselves by keeping the Law. Some really wanted to please God, however, in the flesh, no man can please God. If a man does not choose the road of faith, he is on a dead-end path no matter how nice and appealing the way looks.

> **"There is a way which seems right to a man, but its end is the way of death."** (Proverbs 14:12)

To find the true path to God, the path of faith, a man has to humble himself and acknowledge that his own way will not work. He must submit to God's Word and simply trust Him. The nation of Israel, for the most part, refused to do that. They decided to attempt to keep the Law in order to make themselves righteous before God. Here's the problem with that. The purpose of the Law was always to lead people to faith in God. It was never intended to make a person righteous by keeping it. The Law reveals our sin and drives us to turn from our sin to God, who alone saves. This passage gives mankind two choices. We can either accept the finished work of Christ, and by faith in Him find eternal life, or we can try to do it all our way by attempting to be good enough for God to accept us. Option two has never worked and never will. Unfortunately, as this passage says about Israel,

> **"They did not subject themselves to the righteousness of God." (Vs. 3)**

No one can or ever will save themselves by their own efforts. If a person could, why did Jesus come and die for the sins of the world?

True righteousness comes by faith in God, not by man's works (5-13)

Righteousness and Faith

The primary difference between Christianity and other religions is how a person becomes right with God. Most religions have a set of rules or laws or paths that their followers must adhere to in order to find peace with God. Christianity has only one way, faith. We trust in the death and resurrection of Christ. No human effort can substitute for the blood of Christ. It has been said that religion, by definition, is man's search for God. Christianity is God's search for man. Jesus said He came to seek and save those who are lost. The Pharisees in Jesus' time were religious. Jesus condemned them for trying to earn their righteousness by their good works. The thief on the cross next to Jesus simply acknowledged his sin and said one word to Jesus that saved him. That word was "Lord." He believed and that was all that was needed to receive the promise that Jesus would take him to paradise. Being in right relationship with God (true righteousness) comes by faith and faith alone.

5 For Moses writes that the man who practices the righteousness which is based on law shall live by that righteousness.

If a man decides that he will be saved by keeping the Law of God, then he must keep all the Law and keep it perfectly. Many Scriptures show us that this is impossible. Paul's point is simply that if a man chooses to obey the Law for the purpose of obtaining righteousness, then he is condemned to a life of slavery under the Law. Only faith in Christ can break those chains and set us free.

The nation of Israel was saying "Do!" God is saying "Done!"

> [2] **"For the law of the Spirit of life in Christ Jesus has set you free from the law of sin and of death. [3] For what the Law could not do, weak as it was through the flesh, God did: sending His own Son in the likeness of sinful flesh and as an offering for sin, He condemned sin in the flesh, [4] so that the requirement of the Law might be fulfilled in us, who do not walk according to the flesh but according to the Spirit."** (Romans 8:2-4)

Put another way, this passage is saying:

- **First**. The man who pursues salvation by trying to keep the Law will be judged on the basis of that effort.

- **Second**. It is impossible to keep all the Law.

- **Third**. The inevitable failure of works righteousness results in eternal damnation." *(Austin Precepts commentary)*

6 But the righteousness based on faith speaks as follows: "DO NOT SAY IN YOUR HEART, 'WHO WILL ASCEND INTO HEAVEN?' (THAT IS, TO BRING CHRIST DOWN), **7** or 'WHO WILL DESCEND INTO THE ABYSS?' (THAT IS, TO BRING CHRIST UP FROM THE DEAD)."

The wording of these two verses may sound a bit confusing when you first read them. The thought being expressed is this: We are made righteous by faith. Faith is believing without seeing. It is not necessary to go to Heaven to find Jesus and bring Him here to show us the way. He has already been here and died for our sins and descended to Sheol. After three days, He rose victoriously and later ascended to Heaven. We don't need to bring Him back to find eternal life. We simply believe what He said while He was here and trust Him.

> **"But the way of getting right with God through faith says, "You don't need to go to heaven" (to find Christ and bring him down to help you)."** (New Living Translation: Verse 6)

Paul is actually referring to something Moses said in Deuteronomy that the Jewish people were very familiar with.

> **"For this commandment which I command you today is not too difficult for you, nor is it out of reach. 12 "It is not in heaven, that you should say, 'Who will go up to heaven for us to get it for us and make us hear it, that we may observe it?' 13 "Nor is it beyond the sea, that you should say, 'Who will cross the sea for us to get it for us and make us hear it, that we may observe it?' 14 "But the word is very near you, in your mouth and in your heart, that you may observe it."** (Deuteronomy 30:11-14)

When Paul talks about "ascending" and "descending," he is talking about a man running here and there, searching high and low trying to find the way to eternal life. The point is "The search is over." We don't need to look high and low to find life, to be righteous with God. He has not hidden it in Heaven or the depths of the sea. It was displayed openly on a wooden cross. By faith we all have access. It is not about searching all over for it, but trusting in the One who came searching for us and finished the work.

Faith. That is all it takes, simple faith. All the efforts of man to attain righteousness are futile, empty pursuits. Simply put, salvation is as close to you as a simple prayer of faith. You don't need to go anywhere else to find it.

After talking about how not to find peace with God, Paul will now explain clearly how a person does find that rela-

tionship with God. He begins with saying how close God actually is.

8 But what does it say? "THE WORD IS NEAR YOU, IN YOUR MOUTH AND IN YOUR HEART"—THAT IS, THE WORD of faith which we are preaching, **9** that if you confess with your mouth Jesus as Lord, and believe in your heart that God raised Him from the dead, you will be saved; **10** for with the heart a person believes, resulting in righteousness, and with the mouth he confesses, resulting in salvation. **11** For the Scripture says, "WHOEVER BELIEVES IN HIM WILL NOT BE DISAPPOINTED." **12** For there is no distinction between Jew and Greek; for the same Lord is Lord of all, abounding in riches for all who call on Him; **13** for "WHOEVER WILL CALL ON THE NAME OF THE LORD WILL BE SAVED."

When you think of the mindset of the first-century Jewish community, this had to be one of the most revolutionary things they had ever heard. The concept of salvation, having peace with God, was from the beginning meant to be about faith in God. Period. Many had become polluted with a system of works and religious practices. They had replaced simple faith in God with a complicated system of impossible demands. For many, God had become distant. That is why in the previous verses, Paul tells the people they didn't need to look all over, from Heaven to hell, from east to west, to find the answer. It was nearby all along. Neither was it complicated nor confusing. The answer is, and always has been, simple faith in God.

Here is the message. The Word of God is truth and available to all of us. Jesus Christ died on the cross for our sins, was buried and rose from the dead. He did everything necessary to purchase salvation for every man and woman. All we need to do is genuinely believe it in our hearts, and then publicly take our stand **(Verse 10)** for the One who died for us and gave everything, so we could be His child and inherit everything as His family. *"For with the heart a person believes, resulting in righteousness, and with the mouth he confesses, resulting in salvation."* This amazing passage continues to show that this wonderful salvation is for everyone, "For there is no distinction between Jew and Greek."

Sadly, even today, many try to add to this simple promise by adding other requirements and rules to follow. They say we have to join a particular group, read a certain version of the Bible, serve the church in a particular fashion, wear special clothing or follow particular observances. To all those who insist it is faith plus this or faith plus that, the scripture is loud and clear, **"WHOEVER WILL CALL ON THE NAME OF THE LORD WILL BE SAVED."**

Did you notice that statement was a quote from the Old Testament?

> **"And it will come about that whoever calls on the name of the Lord Will be delivered."** (Joel 2:32)

It was always the same story. Salvation in the Old Testament was always by faith.

> *"Behold, as for the proud one, His soul is not right within him;* **But the righteous will live by his faith."** (Habakkuk 2:4)

> **"Now faith is t**he assurance of things hoped for, the conviction of things not seen. ²**For by it the men of old gained approval."** (Hebrews 11:1, 2)

Remember the three objection in **Chapter 9** that many in Israel charged against God? Think of them in light of what we see about God in **Romans 10:8-13**.

THE FIRST OBJECTION — The Word of God has failed.

Every promise and prophecy concerning the Savior, who would come into the world, to pay for our sins was fulfilled. Every prediction, even the very place He would be born was foretold and fulfilled. Remember what the resurrected Jesus told the two on the road to Emmaus:

> [25] And He said to them, "O foolish men and slow of heart to believe in all that the prophets have spoken! [26] Was it not necessary for the Christ to suffer these things and to enter into His glory?" [27] Then beginning with Moses and with all the prophets, He explained to them the things concerning Himself in all the Scriptures. (Luke 24:25-27)

No, the Word of God has not failed. He has remained true to His Word from the beginning and always will.

THE SECOND OBJECTION — God is unjust

For anyone to charge God with being unjust is simply an admission that they don't know much about God. Consider the evidence. God created a world and mankind by His own sovereign choice. God didn't have to create anything. He doesn't need anything. It was out of love that He shared Himself with a created people that were given free will. He provided everything to show His glory and to provide for His creation. He is infinite in every single glorious attribute, but at His very core, He is Holy. His perfection of being radiates like a trillion suns, and there is no darkness of any kind in Him.

We are not like that. We are sinful by choice and guilty before Him. Every sin is an absolute abhorrence to our Holy God. God, by nature, is repulsed by sin. His reaction is wrath, because sin completely violates every part of His Holiness. He could have slammed the door of Heaven after the first sin and destroyed the world in Holy fury. He would have been totally righteous. However, God did the unthinkable. He sent His Son to be one of us, but without sin. He then sent His Son to the cruel cross to take our place, to literally become our sin on the cross. He poured out His infinite wrath on His own Son. He paid a debt He didn't owe, so we could have a life we don't deserve. His perfect justice was satisfied when the debt was paid by His Son, Jesus Christ.

How can anyone who understands God, and what He has done, ever call Him unjust?

Paul reminds Israel that their charge against God is without merit. If God pardoned a prisoner on death row and didn't pardon a second criminal, does that make God unjust? God is sovereign and can pardon anyone He wishes. He can show grace to anyone He chooses. No one can complain that He is unjust. If God pardoned Jacob and not Esau, it does not make God unjust. All have sinned and fall short of the Glory of God. If He pardons any one of them, then God is gracious, not unjust. The clay cannot tell the potter what to make. The potter knows so much more than the clay could ever understand. He does everything right. He is God. He is never unjust.

THE THIRD OBJECTION — We are not responsible for our actions since God made us the way we are.
When a lost man stands before God at the White Throne Judgment, he will not be sent into a hopeless eternity because he was predestined for hell and had no choice. He will be judged based on his life and how he lived, and the decisions he made concerning Christ.

> [11] **"Then I saw a great white throne and Him who sat upon it, from whose presence earth and heaven fled**

away, and no place was found for them. ¹² **And I saw the dead, the great and the small, standing before the throne, and books were opened; and another book was opened, which is the book of life; and the dead were judged from the things which were written in the books, according to their deeds. ¹³ And the sea gave up the dead which were in it, and death and Hades gave up the dead which were in them; and they were judged, every one of them according to their deeds. ¹⁴ Then death and Hades were thrown into the lake of fire. This is the second death, the lake of fire. ¹⁵ And if anyone's name was not found written in the book of life, he was thrown into the lake of fire."**

(Revelation 20:11-15)

This passage along with numerous others is very clear. We are each responsible for our decisions and the lives we choose to live. The third objection of the nation of Israel is not true. **Romans 10** is all about the responsibility of man. **Verses 8-13** reveal that a person is saved by responding to the Gospel. He has only to call on the Lord and believe on His name. If a person rejects God's salvation, he only has himself to blame, not God.

Paul reminded the Jews in **Chapter 9** of all the privileges God had given them. They had squandered those privileges. They had the Law, the Temple, the priests, the prophets, the promises, the patriarchs, the miracles and protections of God. They literally had the truths of God in their hearts and mouths. That is what Paul is saying in **Verse 8**:

> **"But what does it say? "The word is near you, in your mouth and in your heart"—that is, the word of faith which we are preaching,"** (Romans 10:8)

It was there all along. All that was required of them was to believe God, to have faith in Him. So near, yet they chose to remain far from Him.

What was required of man to do? Confess that Jesus is Lord,

and that God raised Him from the dead. We must believe the Gospel message and make a stand for Christ. The word "confess" in Greek is a legal term which carries with it a public declaration that is binding and contains legal authority. It is not a trivial statement, but a decision that is bound for eternity.

It is a commitment of faith with no reservations.

> **"I will also speak of Your testimonies before kings and shall not be ashamed."** (Psalm 119:46)

Also, of note, is the connection between what we say and what we do. The confession is a commitment like a wedding vow. Paul warned Titus of people that had the right words, but their lives showed no evidence of good deeds. Ephesians and James agree. This true confession produces true works as evidence of that faith.

> [15] **"To the pure, all things are pure; but to those who are defiled and unbelieving, nothing is pure, but both their mind and their conscience are defiled.** [16] **They profess to know God, but by their deeds they deny Him, being detestable and disobedient and worthless for any good deed."**
> (Titus 1:15, 16)

This passage teaches that this salvation offer is for all, Jew and Gentile. **"WHOEVER WILL CALL ON THE NAME OF THE LORD WILL BE SAVED."**

One day, as we know, every tongue will confess that Christ is Lord, but it will be too late for those who did not do it in this lifetime.

> [9] **"God highly exalted Him, and bestowed on Him the name which is above every name,** [10] **so that at the name of Jesus every knee will bow, of those who are in heaven and on earth and under the earth,** [11] **and that every tongue will**

confess that Jesus Christ is Lord, to the glory of God the Father." (Philippians 2:9-11)

The Gospel must be preached (14-15)

14 How then will they call on Him in whom they have not believed? How will they believe in Him whom they have not heard? And how will they hear without a preacher? **15** How will they preach unless they are sent? Just as it is written, "HOW BEAUTIFUL ARE THE FEET OF THOSE WHO BRING GOOD NEWS OF GOOD THINGS!"

A wonderful song of testimony picks up the story of these verses:

> **"I was dead when I was born,**
> **Soul bound up in chain**
> **Didn't have the will to think,**
> **That I could ever change**
> **Then in love my brother came,**
> **And set my poor heart free**
> **How beautiful the feet that brought good news to me"**
>
> (How Beautiful the Feet, by Max Butler)

A now-famous conversation took place in England in the 18th century when William Carey, often called the father of modern missions, was presenting his desire to take the Gospel to the land of India. One of the elders in his church told him, "Sit down young man. If God wants to convert the heathen He will do it without your help or mine." Of course, as we know, William Carey chose to believe the words of **Romans 10** and many other passages. Even without the support of his church, he went on to become one of the world's greatest missionaries.

In **Chapter 9,** I described a puzzle no man can solve. Is God sovereign? Yes, as we saw in **Chapter 9.** Does God elect?   Does man have to hear the message? Heed the message? Believe the message?" Yes, according to this passage. If man rejects the message, will he be responsible for his decision? Yes. Yes, to each of these points.

Chapter 9 focused on the Sovereignty of God. **Chapter 10,** the role and responsibility of man. Let's now look at man's part.

Romans 1 introduced the Gospel as "the power of God for salvation to everyone who believes, to the Jew first and also to the Greek" **(Romans 1:16).** What good is it if nobody hears it?

Does God write the Gospel in the stars so that men all over the world have only to look up and be saved? Does God send His angels forth with a loud voice calling all to repent? How does God get His Gospel out to everyone so they can hear it and believe the good news?

The answer is simply stated in **Romans 10:14-17.** It teaches:

- Salvation comes when a person believes in Christ and calls on His name to be saved.
- A person must first hear the good news of the Gospel from someone.
- Someone must go to the lost and proclaim the Gospel message to them.
- The believers, the Church, the body of Christ, are responsible to make sure that someone takes the Gospel message to the lost world.
- It all fulfills the final command of Christ to take the Gospel message to Jerusalem, Judea, Samaria and the furthest regions of the world (**Acts 1:8**).

For an elder of a church or anyone to suggest that God will convert the heathen without anyone's participation, is completely wrong. God, of course, could do anything He wants, but what He has decreed is to use man to spread the message of Christ's death and resurrection. That is His sovereign, clearly stated way to get His gracious message out to an unbelieving world.

Allow me to tell a personal story. For many years, I was a professional firefighter in San Diego, California. On more than one occasion, we had to enter a dark, hot, burning building to search for people who were trapped. When the call came in, we had to respond as quickly as possible. There was no time to hesitate when lives are at risk. What if a fireman didn't want to go in? Maybe he was scared. What if he didn't want to disturb the people still asleep in the burning building? You would probably answer these ridiculous excuses with "Just go in, do your job, find the people and lead them out of danger and into safety!" What is the difference between that and sharing the Gospel? All believers have the call, and we have the only message that can bring a soul that is in darkness into safety, the eternal light of Christ.

This entire section is a call to personal responsibility. Everyone is personally responsible. The church is responsible to make sure they are training and sending. The ones sent are responsible to fulfill their calling and proclaim the Gospel message to the lost. The lost are responsible to call upon the Lord to be saved.

Remember when Cornelius, the Roman Centurion, was given a vision and told by angels that he had to send for Peter. We see in this passage how God uses people and the spoken word to bring people to salvation.

> [13] "And he reported to us how he had seen the angel standing in his house, and saying, 'Send to Joppa and have Simon, who is also called Peter, brought here; [14] and he will speak words to you by which you will be saved, you and all your household." (Acts 11:13, 14)

Many in Israel rejected the Gospel (16-21)

16 However, they did not all heed the good news; for Isaiah says, "LORD, WHO HAS BELIEVED OUR REPORT?" **17** So faith *comes* from hearing, and hearing by the word of Christ.

18 But I say, surely they have never heard, have they? Indeed, they have;

"THEIR VOICE HAS GONE OUT INTO ALL THE EARTH,
AND THEIR WORDS TO THE ENDS OF THE WORLD."

19 But I say, surely Israel did not know, did they? First Moses says,

"I WILL MAKE YOU JEALOUS BY THAT WHICH IS NOT A NATION,
BY A NATION WITHOUT UNDERSTANDING WILL I ANGER YOU."

20 And Isaiah is very bold and says,

"I WAS FOUND BY THOSE WHO DID NOT SEEK ME,
I BECAME MANIFEST TO THOSE WHO DID NOT ASK FOR ME."

21 But as for Israel He says, "ALL THE DAY LONG I HAVE STRETCHED OUT MY HANDS TO A DISOBEDIENT AND OBSTINATE PEOPLE."

Chapter 9 listed three unsubstantiated complaints Israel had against God. This concluding portion of **Chapter 10** now records **two more complaints**. Paul will then answer each argument with a quotation from the Old Testament to disprove the complaints.

COMPLAINT NUMBER ONE – You say salvation comes only through faith in God. We have not heard this before now.

Paul is very clear that God's message had gone out *"into all the earth, And their words to the ends of the world."* God had spoken through Moses and the prophets clearly in many ways and times.

God had also made Himself known in the created world by displaying His glory and providing for all of man's needs.

> **"Because that which is known about God is evident within them; for God made it evident to them. [20] For since the creation of the world His invisible attributes, His eternal power and divine nature, have been clearly seen, being understood through what has been made, so that they are without excuse."** (Romans 1:19, 20)

God had also put His Law in the heart of every man, even the most remote heathen people. In essence, all people, Jew and pagan, have these outward and inward evidences of a moral Creator.

> [14] **"For when Gentiles who do not have the Law do instinctively the things of the Law, these, not having the Law, are a law to themselves, [15] in that they show the work of the Law written in their hearts, their conscience bearing witness and their thoughts alternately accusing or else defending them."** (Romans 2:14, 15)

Israel understood so much more. They had a long history of God's special prophets to guide them along the way and protect them. They had all the pictures of salvation in the temple, priests, and feasts. They had everything.

> **"And the LORD has sent to you all His servants the prophets again and again, but you have not listened nor inclined your ear to hear,"** (Jeremiah 25:4)

And the words of Jesus Himself:

> **"O Jerusalem, Jerusalem, who kills the prophets and stones those who are sent to her! How often I wanted to gather your children together, the way a hen gathers her chicks under her wings, and you were unwilling."**
> (Matthew 23:37)

God had spoken clearly to ancient Israel. They had heard His Words. They chose instead to live by the Law, and now they are perishing by the Law. The way of faith had been in front of them all the time.

COMPLAINT NUMBER TWO - This message is not one we understand. God did not communicate it clearly to us.

They not only had heard, but they understood as well. Because of their rejection, God sent His message to the Gentiles who would listen and believe. He then quotes both Moses and Isaiah and tells them that they rejected God in spite of all He had done to bring them to Himself. The Lord even said He would provoke them to jealousy and anger by inviting others to His feast. It was to show the Jews it was about grace, not something they earn. It was to bring them back to their senses and repentance.

In the end, all God could say to His rebellious nation was the final condemnation found in **Verse 21:**

> **"ALL THE DAY LONG I HAVE STRETCHED OUT MY HANDS TO A DISOBEDIENT AND OBSTINATE PEOPLE."**

This is that verse in the Amplified Bible:

> **"But of Israel he says, All day long I have stretched out
> My hands to a people unyielding and disobedient and
> self-willed [to a faultfinding, contrary, and contradicting
> people]."** (Romans 10:21 Amplified Bible)

Israel had a long history of being stubborn and obstinate. Listen to what God instructed Moses to tell the people centuries before:

> **"Know, then, it is not because of your righteousness that
> the LORD your God is giving you this good land to possess,
> for you are a stubborn people. Remember, do not forget
> how you provoked the LORD your God to wrath in the wilderness; from the day that you left the land of Egypt until
> you arrived at this place, you have been rebellious against
> the LORD."** (Deuteronomy 9:6, 7)

Romans 10 is a rebuke to Israel for their continued stubbornness and worn out excuses. It is a clear explanation of how a person comes to true faith. We each have responsibilities to carry that Gospel message to those who have not yet heard.

Chapter 11 looks forward to a day when all of God's children, both believing Jew and believing Gentile will be brought together into one community of Faith. We will look at that next.

Romans Chapter 11

Israel has not been rejected,
a remnant remains.

"Branches were
broken off so that I
might be grafted in."
(Romans 11:19)

CHAPTER OVERVIEW

Chapter 11 concludes the three chapters Paul set aside to specifically address the nation of Israel. The big issue Paul was dealing with was that God had not rejected His people, Israel. That theme will carry throughout the entire chapter.

Many in Israel through the ages rejected God. They have faced the judgment of God. He has always had a believing remnant who have remained true to the faith. One of the important images in this chapter that portrays Israel, the Gentiles and the Kingdom of God, is the olive tree. The remnant of Jewish believers along with believing Gentiles now make up the Kingdom of God on earth, the complete flourishing olive tree.

THE KEY VERSE FOR CHAPTER 11

> 24 **"For if you were cut off from what is by nature a wild olive tree, and were grafted contrary to nature into a cultivated olive tree, how much more will these who are the natural branches be grafted into their own olive tree?"**

SIMPLE OUTLINE

I. Romans 11:1-16 - Israel has not been rejected, a remnant remains.

II. Romans 11:17-24 - The parable of the two olive trees.

III. Romans 11:25-32 - The future hope for true Israel, the Remnant.

IV. Romans 11:33-36 - Song of praise to our unfathomable God.

Romans 11 Commentary

Israel has not been rejected, a remnant remains (11:1-16)

1 I say then, God has not rejected His people, has He? May it never be! For I too am an Israelite, a descendant of Abraham, of the tribe of Benjamin. **2** God has not rejected His people whom He foreknew. Or do you not know what the Scripture says in *the passage about* Elijah, how he pleads with God against Israel? **3** "Lord, THEY HAVE KILLED YOUR PROPHETS, THEY HAVE TORN DOWN YOUR ALTARS, AND I ALONE AM LEFT, AND THEY ARE SEEKING MY LIFE." **4** But what is the divine response to him? "I HAVE KEPT FOR MYSELF SEVEN THOUSAND MEN WHO HAVE NOT BOWED THE KNEE TO BAAL." **5** In the same way then, there has also come to be at the present time a remnant according to *God's* gracious choice. **6** But if it is by grace, it is no longer on the basis of works, otherwise, grace is no longer grace.

7 What then? What Israel is seeking, it has not obtained, but those who were chosen obtained it, and the rest were hardened; **8** just as it is written,

"GOD GAVE THEM A SPIRIT OF STUPOR,
EYES TO SEE NOT AND EARS TO HEAR NOT,
DOWN TO THIS VERY DAY."

9 And David says,"LET THEIR TABLE BECOME A SNARE AND A TRAP, AND A STUMBLING BLOCK AND A RETRIBUTION TO THEM. **10** "LET THEIR EYES BE DARKENED TO SEE NOT, AND BEND THEIR BACKS FOREVER." **11** I say then, they did not stumble so as to fall, did they? May it never be! But by their transgression salvation *has come* to the Gentiles, to make them jealous. **12** Now if their transgression is riches for the world and their failure is riches for the Gentiles, how much more will their fulfillment be! **13** But I am speaking to you who are Gentiles. Inasmuch then as I am an apostle of Gentiles, I magnify my ministry, **14** if somehow I might move to jealousy my fellow countrymen and save some of them. **15** For if their rejection is the reconciliation of the world, what will *their* acceptance be but life from the dead? **16** If the first piece *of dough* is holy, the lump is also; and if the root is holy, the branches are too.

ROMANS 11:1-6 THREE PIECES OF EVIDENCE ARE PRESENTED TO PROVE THAT GOD RESTORES THOSE WHO WILL RETURN TO HIM.

Let's begin with the last verse of **Chapter 10**.

> **"But as for Israel He says, "ALL THE DAY LONG I HAVE STRETCHED OUT MY HANDS TO A DISOBEDIENT AND OBSTINATE PEOPLE."** (Romans 10:21)

It is clear that God has shown great patience with His chosen people. He has continuously reached out for them, stretched out His hands. **Chapter 11** picks it up from there. Paul will list three pieces of evidence proving that God has not abandoned His stubborn people.

1 I say then, God has not rejected His people, has He? May it never be! For I too am an Israelite, a descendant of Abraham, of the tribe of Benjamin.

FIRST EVIDENCE — Paul himself.

Paul presents himself as the first piece of supporting evidence that God has not given up on Israel. Paul was a Pharisee of Pharisees, a key leader in the nation of Israel. In his zeal he even persecuted the church and put some to death. God interrupted his path of destruction. He was put on a true path to God. Paul, by the grace of God, was saved from a life of works-righteousness into a life of faith. If God can do that to Paul, then He can do it for anyone.

2 God has not rejected His people whom He foreknew. Or do you not know what the Scripture says in the passage about Elijah, how he pleads with God against Israel? **3** "Lord, THEY HAVE KILLED YOUR PROPHETS, THEY HAVE TORN DOWN YOUR ALTARS, AND I ALONE AM LEFT, AND THEY ARE SEEKING MY LIFE." **4** But what is the divine response to him? "I HAVE KEPT FOR MYSELF SEVEN THOUSAND MEN WHO HAVE NOT BOWED THE KNEE TO BAAL."

SECOND EVIDENCE — Elijah.

Paul now reminds Israel of God's sovereignty and calling by quoting passages from the story of the prophet Elijah. He quotes two passages from **1 Kings 19**. Elijah was being chased by Jezebel and now was hiding. He felt he had done all God asked him to do and feared for his life. He complained to God that God had given up on His people and only Elijah was left (**1 Kings 19:10**). God told His prophet that he was not alone.

There were 7,000 true believers in the country that God had preserved **(1 Kings 19:18)**. He had His remnant even during times of persecution and darkness that had overrun the land.

The point of this defense was to remind Israel that even when they wandered from God, He never left them. His watchful eye was always on them.

When you see evil in the world today, and it seems like everyone is going the wrong way. D you sometimes think you are alone? Remeber this, you are not alone.

5 In the same way then, there has also come to be at the present time a remnant according to *God's* gracious choice. **6** But if it is by grace, it is no longer on the basis of works, otherwise, grace is no longer grace.

THIRD EVIDENCE —**There remains a remnant by the grace of God, not because of human works.**

Paul's third appeal to the nation of Israel is to consider the great all-knowing and all-loving God. It is God who has chosen Israel to be the channel of the Messiah. This choice was not determined by how good or faithful Israel would be or how many good works they were to do. It was a sovereign choice of God and is based on His grace alone. In light of that, how can Israel say that God has reversed His sovereign choice. God has kept a believing remnant like Paul, Elijah, and others in the land because of His great love and grace. Grace is not connected to any work. It is only connected to God. Since the remnant exists because they are a work of God, they will continue to exist. They are true, believing Israel.

What about those who have not remained faithful? Why have so many deserted? Why has this happened? **Verses 7-10** deal with this question.

Romans 11: 7-10 Understanding the hardening, in part, of Israel

7 What then? What Israel is seeking, it has not obtained, but those who were chosen obtained it, and the rest were hardened;

Paul presents evidence that God will save even the most rebellious of Israel if they will repent. He then focuses on those who reject God's offer of reconciliation. Their hearts have become hardened, like Pharaoh in **Romans 9.** Pharaoh both hardened his own heart and God hardened his heart. The Jews both hardened their hearts to God and God hardened their hearts. God is both loving and sovereign. He is also exceedingly patient with His disobedient and stubborn people.

Paul then quotes two Old Testament Scriptures that predict the hardening of Israel.

8 just as it is written,

"GOD GAVE THEM A SPIRIT OF STUPOR,
EYES TO SEE NOT AND EARS TO HEAR NOT,
DOWN TO THIS VERY DAY." *(Isaiah 29:10)*

9 And David says,

"LET THEIR TABLE BECOME A SNARE AND A TRAP,

Why would God do this to His chosen people? We have already seen that God has not abandoned or deserted Israel. What was He doing to them and why?

Every parent has to deal with the issue of what to do with a child that disobeys. If the problem is allowed to continue, the child will grow up unable to function in society. But even worse, the child will not obey the Word of God. If they disobey their human father, they will do the same with our Heavenly Father. That is why God exhorts parents to discipline their children. As hard as discipline is at the moment, it results in long-lasting benefits in the life of the child.

> **"All discipline for the moment seems not to be joyful, but sorrowful; yet to those who have been trained by it, afterwards it yields the peaceful fruit of righteousness."**
> (Hebrews 12:11)

Israel was a disobedient child that God had to discipline. Some of the measures God used were severe. It was always to help His wayward child. This passage describes one such type of discipline, jealousy.

Remember, this entire section of Scripture, which deals directly with Israel, began in **Chapter 9.** Paul addresses three major complaints by the people of Israel. They complained that the **Word of God had failed**, **God was unjust**, and because of this, **they were not responsible for their actions**. Now, Paul once again deals with these issues when he discusses the hardening of the people of God over the centuries. He shows that God chose them even though He knew they would fail Him. **Romans 11:2** is clear that it was not God who first rejected His people. Even God, has a limit concerning the rejection of His people after He had done so much for them. In **Romans 1,** we saw how the heathen had rejected God as their maker. He gave them over to greater sin. It was the fruit of their rejection. Now, God has turned His holy judgment on His people Israel. Since they have turned their eyes away from God, He now blinds their eyes. Since they stopped listening to their God, He now deafens their ears. In all of it, His desire is for Israel to bend their knee and return to God. God's discipline of His erring people is severe.

Remember the man living in sin in **1 Corinthians 5**? Paul's instruction was also severe. There was hope it would bring the man back to God. In **2 Corinthians** we see that it worked.

> **¹ "It is actually reported that there is immorality among you, and immorality of such a kind as does not exist even among the Gentiles, that someone has his father's wife. ² You have become arrogant and have not mourned instead, so that the one who had done this deed would be removed from your midst. ³ For I, on my part, though absent in body but present in spirit, have already judged him who has so committed this, as though I were present. ⁴ In the name of our Lord Jesus, when you are assembled, and I with you in spirit, with the power of our Lord Jesus, ⁵ I have decided to deliver such a one to Satan for the destruction of his flesh, so that his spirit may be saved in the day of the Lord Jesus."** (1 Corinthians 5:1-5)

Paul treated the sin in Corinth the same way God dealt with the sin of His people Israel who had become unfaithful to Him when they chased after other gods. The purpose in both instances was the same, to ultimately drive the people back to faith in God.

This stubbornness and hardness of heart is found throughout the Scripture, both Old, and New Testament. The following are a few of the passages from the prophets to the Gospels and the words of Jesus, Himself.

- **Romans 11:8** "as it is written, 'God gave them a spirit of stupor, eyes that would not see and ears that would not hear, down to this very day.'"

- **Deuteronomy 29:4** "But to this day the Lord has not given you the heart to understand or eyes to see or ears to hear."

- **Isaiah 29:10** "For the Lord has poured out upon you a spirit of deep sleep, and has closed your eyes (the prophets), and covered your heads (the seers)."

- **2 Corinthians 3:14-15** "But their minds were hardened. For to this day, when they read the old covenant, that same veil remains unlifted, because only through Christ is it taken away. Yes, to this day whenever Moses is read a veil lies over their hearts."

- **Matthew 13:13-14** "This is why I speak to them in parables, because seeing they do not see, and hearing they do not hear, nor do they understand. Indeed, in their case, the prophecy of Isaiah is fulfilled that says: 'You will indeed hear but never understand, and you will indeed see but never perceive.'"

- **Ezekiel 12:2** "Son of man, you dwell in the midst of a rebellious house, who have eyes to see, but see not, who have ears to hear, but hear not, for they are a rebellious house."

- And many more passages. See also **Jeremiah 11:17, Jeremiah 5:21, Acts 28:26, Mark 4:11-12, 2 Kings 17:34, 2 Kings 17:41, Isaiah 6:9.**

The warnings to Israel were clear and abundant. Disobedience brings strong consequences. We are seeing in all this both the kindness and the severity of God.

This next section will deal with that. Let us look at **Verse 22** as a summary of **Verses 8-10**

> [22] **"Behold then the kindness and severity of God; to those who fell, severity, but to you, God's kindness, if you continue in His kindness; otherwise you also will be cut off."**

There was more. Not only did God use severe measures to bring His people back, He also used the stumbling of Israel to open the doors of salvation for the Gentiles.

Romans 11: 11-16 – An open door for the Gentiles

11 I say then, they did not stumble so as to fall, did they? May it never be! But by their transgression salvation *has come* to the Gentiles, to make them jealous.

Before we consider the Gentiles, we need to think for a moment what it meant that God used "jealousy" as a way to bring the children of Israel back home to Himself.

DISCIPLINE BY JEALOUSY

The Greek word translated "jealousy" means to stir someone out of complacency to take action, and to become more like the one they are envying. It meant God intended to make His people want to change their behavior by seeing the benefits of better behavior.

God wanted His people Israel to come back to Him. He used every means to accomplish that, even making them jealous of His pardoning the Gentiles who repented. To have the blessings of Jacob again, they had to stop living like Esau.

You can see this clearly in reading this passage in the Amplified Bible:

> 11 "So I say, have they stumbled so as to fall [to spiritual ruin]? Certainly not! But by their transgression [their rejection of the Messiah] salvation has come to the Gentiles, to make Israel jealous [when they realize what they have forfeited]. 12 Now if Israel's transgression means riches for the world [at large] and their failure means riches for the Gentiles, how much more will their fulfillment and reinstatement be! 13 But now I am speaking to you who are Gentiles. Inasmuch then as I am an apostle to the Gentiles, I magnify my ministry, 14 in the hope of somehow making my fellow countrymen jealous [by stirring them up so that they will seek the truth] and perhaps save some of them. 15 For if their [present] rejection [of salvation] is for the reconciliation of the world [to God], what will their acceptance [of salvation] be but [nothing less than] life from the dead?"   Romans 11:11-15 (The Amplified Bible)

It was not only to bring Israel home, but to bring all of His children into the family. Let's look at the Gentiles in this section.

12 Now if their transgression is riches for the world and their failure is riches for the Gentiles, how much more will their fulfillment be!

God's thoughts are higher than the heavens, His ways past finding out. What begins as a great betrayal by Israel, will be used by God to build a highway of salvation for the Gentile nations. Only God can bring beauty out of ashes.

> "To all who mourn in Israel,
>> he will give a crown of beauty for ashes,

a joyous blessing instead of mourning,
    festive praise instead of despair.
In their righteousness, they will be like great oaks
    that the LORD HAS PLANTED FOR HIS OWN GLORY."
(New Living Translation, Isaiah 61:3)

The Almighty alone can make all things work together for good for those He calls according to His purpose **(Romans 8:28)**. The point of Paul's argument is that if God did the amazing thing of bringing the Gentiles into His family because the Jews rejected the special privilege that had been given them, then just imagine if His chosen people repented and returned to God. Can't you just see the prodigal's father standing in the doorway with tears in his eyes, waiting for his wayward son to come home? Imagine the great feast awaiting him when he returns to his Father.

HELPFUL INSIGHT

A beautiful Greek word used in **Verse 12** adds a wonderful shade of meaning to understand the very heart of God. The word translated "fullness" is *plērōma.* The word is used to describe a ship's cargo hold being completely filled with merchandise. Ancient Greeks used the word to describe a ship ready to sail, when the last crew member and soldier were on board. Also, when an entire family was together, it was *plērōma*, complete, nobody missing, nothing lacking. In **Verse 12**, The body of Christ will not be *plērōma* (complete) until all of God's children are home safe, which includes the believing Gentiles and the Jewish Remnant. This verse proclaims, what a great day of blessing that will be for all.

> [12] **"Now if their transgression is riches for the world and their failure is riches for the Gentiles, how much more will their fulfillment (***plērōma)* **be!"**

We will see that word *plērōma* once more in this chapter*:*

> **"For I would not, brethren, that ye should be ignorant of this mystery, lest ye should be wise in your own conceits; that blindness in part is happened to Israel, until the fullness (*plērōma*) of the Gentiles be come in."** (Romans 11:25)

A RETURN TO THE POTTER'S HOUSE

Picking up on the potter's image used in **Chapter 9,** we find a parallel to this passage. A potter who has a ruined vessel on the wheel will usually cut the clay off the wheel and toss the damaged clay aside for a season. It will be stored in a bucket and re-saturated with water, and then when fully soaked, he pounds the clay on a table or board to remove all air and make the clay usable again. The old, ruined clay is then ready to be used again, even mixed with new clay to form a vessel of the potter's design. What was spoiled, now joins new clay and becomes part of the new design. Now combined, both clays, then go through the fire to become a single vessel of beauty.

13 But I am speaking to you who are Gentiles. Inasmuch then as I am an apostle of Gentiles, I magnify my ministry, **14** if somehow I might move to jealousy my fellow countrymen and save some of them. **15** For if their rejection is the reconciliation of the world, what will *their* acceptance be but life from the dead? **16** If the first piece *(First fruit) of dough* is holy, the lump is also *(Numbers (15:17-21);* and if the root is holy, the branches are too.

We see how God is accomplishing this great plan. His rebellious people return and join the believing Gentiles to form one new man. Have you ever seen a family that has a new baby? The older children in that family find themselves in a new position. They used to be the center of attention, but now, the baby takes center stage. Jealousy can result. We once brought home a new daughter from the hospital. When the older daughter first saw her new sister she leaned over the crib. We thought she was giving her a kiss. However, she was actually biting her new sister. Of course, we were all shocked, especially the new baby who had just arrived. Jealousy! Today, they are very close but it was a tough start.

Even though jealousy is a tough strategy to use to bring people back or get them to think, it can be effective. That is what God did. The Gentiles were the new baby, and it caught the attention of the Jews who thought they were the center of God's family. God always wanted a complete family made up of all people. As a parent, I can relate to that desire. We want all our children to live in love and harmony with each other. We have experienced the joy of seeing it happen. Why would we think our Heavenly Father would want anything less. Whatever it takes. Whatever discipline is necessary. In this passage, God uses the rejection of His rebellious people. He provokes them to jealousy in order to bring them home to meet their new family members. The end result is like "life from the dead."

A LUMP OF DOUGH AND AN ANCIENT ROOT – ROMANS 11:16

16 If the first piece *(First fruit) of dough* is holy, the lump is also *(Numbers (15:17-21)*; and if the root is holy, the branches are too.

In **Numbers 15**, God gave instructions to the children of Israel about things they were to do when they entered the Promised Land. The instructions were mainly about the worship and thanksgiving offerings they were to give as a nation. This was to thank God for protecting them and bringing them to the land He promised. These offerings were to continue into the new land as reminders to the people of the great things God had done. The instructions applied to all of Israel and also to the strangers in their midst who followed Israel out of Egypt. The Gentiles were equally included in the blessings of God. They were seen as one people in the eyes of God.

Romans 11:16 refers to a lump of dough and the first fruits that were to be offered to God when the Hebrew children entered the land. Here are the original instructions from **Numbers 15:17-21** that **Romans 11** is referencing:

> "¹⁷ "Then the LORD SPOKE TO MOSES, SAYING, ¹⁸ "Speak to the sons of Israel and say to them, 'When you enter the land where I bring you, ¹⁹ then it shall be, that when you eat of the food of the land, you shall lift up an offering to the LORD. ²⁰ Of the first of your dough you shall lift up a cake as an offering; as the offering of the threshing floor, so you shall lift it up. ²¹ From the first of your dough you shall give to the LORD AN OFFERING THROUGHOUT YOUR GENERATIONS."

The reason for this practice is given at the end of the chapter.

> ⁴⁰ "so that you may remember to do all My commandments and be holy to your God. ⁴¹ I am the LORD YOUR GOD WHO BROUGHT YOU OUT FROM THE LAND OF EGYPT TO BE YOUR GOD; I AM THE LORD YOUR GOD."

From the time the wheat harvest was first gathered, to the time the flour was ground, until the bread dough was formed, it was all offered to God as a first fruits offering. It was an offering of worship and dependence on God to bring the future harvests and blessing. God was acknowledged as the One who blesses and brings the increase.

Romans 11:16 is a reminder that because the first offerings were done in faith and acceptable to God, then the offerings that followed were also holy to God and set apart for Him. Since the people had begun by faith in God, they were children of Abraham, Isaac, and Jacob. They were from the same root stock and the same lump of sanctified dough.

The point of this passage is all who exercised that same faith of Abraham, Isaac, and Jacob were children of Abraham. The great root of the tree remained strong and healthy, even though many Jews had been cut off from the root. There were branches that existed. A remnant remained, a remnant of faith. Living branches growing from that strong root.

The remnant is also described as taken from the sanctified lump of dough. They were set apart for blessing, since they were taken from the same batch of dough that God accepted. These two illustrations, the branch, and the dough teach the same thing. There remains a believing remnant of people from Israel who are actually true Israel. These are joined by believing Gentiles and are one sanctified people.

This, along with the rest of **Romans 11**, affirms the opening question and answer given in **Romans 11:1, "I say then, God has not rejected His people, has He? May it never be!"**

This will be expanded in more detail in the next verses when we examine the parable of the two olive trees.

The parable of the two Olive Trees (Romans 11:17-24)

ISRAEL AND THE OLIVE TREE

The LORD CALLED YOUR NAME,
"A green olive tree, beautiful in fruit and form"
(Jeremiah 11:16)

The **olive tree** is mentioned many times in the Bible, often associated with blessings, fertility, and health. The State of Israel chose the olive tree as its emblem to symbolize peace. It was an olive leaf that a dove from Noah's ark brought to Noah, *"Then the dove came to him in the evening, and behold, a freshly plucked olive leaf was in her mouth; and Noah knew that the waters had receded from the earth"* **(Genesis 8:11)**.

The olive tree is an enduring tree. There are olive trees in the Garden of Gethsemane which are believed to have existed from the time of Jesus. The olive tree is associated with national prosperity. It is a source of income for many in Israel.

God uses the olive tree to represent His Kingdom. A Kingdom made up of the natural branches, true Israel, and the branches grafted in, believing Gentiles, .

Several lessons are learned from the parable of the two olive trees in Romans 11:17-24.

Romans 11:17, 18 – Important lessons for the Gentiles

LESSON 1 — GENTILES HAVE NO REASON FOR ARROGANCE

17 But if some of the branches were broken off, and you, being a wild olive, were grafted in among them and became partaker with them of the rich root of the olive tree *(Jeremiah 11:16),* **18** do not be arrogant toward the branches; but if you are arrogant, *remember that* it is not you who supports the root, but the root *supports* you.

Paul addresses the believing Gentiles as wild olive branches and describes them as being grafted into the root system of the olive tree. It is a work of God, He is the Gardener, not the Gentiles. They did not graft themselves in. They have only God to thank. They have no reason to be prideful or arrogant.

Someone once said, "Pride, or arrogance, is the only disease that makes everyone sick except the one that has it." We have all known boastful and arrogant people. It is difficult to be around them. Paul is warning the Gentiles that they need to avoid this pitfall. When we get to **Chapter 12** we will see that repeated:

> **"For through the grace given to me I say to everyone among you not to think more highly of himself than he ought to think; but to think so as to have sound judgment, as God has allotted to each a measure of faith. "**
>
> (Romans 12:3)

Remember when God called Gideon to defeat the Midianites

with just a handful of men. God told Gideon why He wanted just a few:

> "The LORD said to Gideon, "The people who are with you are too many for Me to give Midian into their hands, for Israel would become boastful, saying, 'My own power has delivered me.' (Judges 7:2)

LESSON 2 — ISRAEL HAS NOT BEEN REPLACED

Another important thing to understand is that the Gentiles being grafted in do not take the place of Israel, the natural branches. Some today believe the church has replaced Israel. That is simply not the case. Believing Gentiles and believing Israel exist together in God's Kingdom on earth. They are one olive tree supported by the foundational root which goes back to Abraham, Isaac, and Jacob. It is one body made up of all true believers.

LESSON 3 — ABOUT ROOTS

Many people like to think about their roots. They research their genealogies to trace their family lines. Some want to find some significant person in their family line and others just want to know about their heritage. Many are looking for some kind of significance. As believers, we also have roots. Our root system, that which sustains our lives, is God Himself.

No member of the kingdom of God should boast in anything other than God. God is our root system, we need never claim any other roots. Being part of God's family is an undeserved privilege. It is all of God. Everything we do is dependent on Him, not our own flesh. Jesus put it this way:

> "As the branch cannot bear fruit of itself unless it abides in the vine, so neither *can* you unless you abide in Me. ⁵ I am the vine, you are the branches; he who abides in Me

and I in him, he bears much fruit, for apart from Me you can do nothing." (John 15:4, 5)

A great hope along with a great warning (verses 19-24)

Paul now continues his warnings in **Verses 19-24**. The Gentiles can cut themselves off from the root just as the Jews did. God is not a respecter of persons. He judges all people fairly and evenly. He plants, He blesses, He uproots, and He judges when people turn away from Him. He is the True Root. No one, Jew or Gentile, can flourish without Him. He is the source of life. Jesus reminded the people of this principle when He said:

> "I am the true vine, and My Father is the vinedresser. [2] Every branch in Me that does not bear fruit, He takes away; and every branch that bears fruit, He prunes it so that it may bear more fruit. [3] You are already clean because of the word which I have spoken to you. [4] Abide in Me, and I in you. As the branch cannot bear fruit of itself unless it abides in the vine, so neither can you unless you abide in Me. [5] I am the vine, you are the branches; he who abides in Me and I in him, he bears much fruit, for apart from Me you can do nothing." (John 15:1-6)

19 You will say then, "Branches were broken off so that I might be grafted in." **20** Quite right, they were broken off for their unbelief, but you stand by your faith. Do not be conceited, but fear; **21** for if God did not spare the natural branches, He will not spare you, either. **22** Behold then the kindness and severity of God; to those who fell, severity, but to you, God's kindness, if you continue in His kindness;

otherwise you also will be cut off. **23** And they also, if they do not continue in their unbelief, will be grafted in, for God is able to graft them in again. **24** For if you were cut off from what is by nature a wild olive tree, and were grafted contrary to nature into a cultivated olive tree, how much more will these who are the natural *branches* be grafted into their own olive tree?

These verses contain great hope as well as a great warning. The hope is that God is faithful to His Word. "Whosoever shall call on the name of the Lord shall be saved." Even those in the nation of Israel, who had cut themselves off can repent and can be grafted back into the root. God offers a great chance to come back to the life of being in Him. If the Gentiles remain faithful to him, they remain connected to the source of life. That is what God wants. It is great hope for all people. Two options are presented to all people, Jew and Gentile. We can all pick from these two options.

KINDNESS AND SEVERITY

[22] "Behold then the kindness and severity of God; to those who fell, severity, but to you, God's kindness, if you continue in His kindness; otherwise you also will be cut off."

Fourteen hundred years before Paul wrote this, God gave the nation of Israel these two exact choices. Not only would the Jewish people reading this in the first century have recognized it, but they also would have been reminded of why the nation of Israel had been under the severity of God for centuries. They would have been reminded of what God had clearly told them in **Leviticus 26**.

Moses warned the people that they had a choice to make. If they followed Him and kept His commandments, they would know His kindness and blessing. If they rejected Him and embraced the idolatry and sin of the world, then they would know His severity, His wrath, and judgment. I highly recommend you read **Leviticus 26**. This is a brief summary of the blessings and curses promised in that chapter to the Jewish people.

Leviticus 26:1-11 — The kindness of God and the blessings if they followed God.

- Their land would be productive - all trees, fruit, and vineyards will flourish. There will always be an abundance of food to eat.
- There will be peace in the land, no more sword or wars, and everyone will live securely.
- All harmful beasts and pestilences will be removed.
- Any nation that attempts to harm them will flee in fear, because God will fight for them.
- God will once again live in their midst and walk among them. They will be His people.
- They would never again be enslaved by any nation.

Leviticus 26:12-46 — The severity of God and the judgments to come if they choose to abandon God.

- Terror and disease will come upon them. Fear will travel with them everywhere.
- Their enemies will again rule over them and treat them harshly.
- Their vines will not produce enough food to eat.
- Wild animals will overrun the land and will kill their children. Great famine and hunger will cover the land.
- Enemies would surround the land. In desperation, they will even eat their children because of hunger.
- God will no longer accept their sacrifices or destroy their cities by foreign armies. Israel will be scattered among the nations.
- They will be taken away from their land by a foreign power. The land will finally enjoy its Sabbath rests.

It is hard to imagine, given these two choices, that the children of Israel would choose the second path. That is exactly what they did and everything God warned would happen, did happen. Much of the Old Testament is about that story.

Romans 11 reminds the Jewish people again what God told them in the time of Moses. If they would repent and turn to their God, then He would restore them. God, like the prodigal's father, always had the light on and was looking out His window for His children to come home.

One final note on the "kindness and severity of God." The verse does not say the kindness and judgment of God. Severity is a description of the most extreme form of discipline of a rebellious child. God uses even the most extreme measures of discipline to bring about repentance of His prodigal children. Discipline is harsh, but it is hopeful. It is not God giving up on Israel, just the opposite. It is God that wants them to return from the pigpen of life, and return back to His forever family. As we will see, some will be restored.

The future hope for true Israel, the remnant (11:25-32)

25 For I do not want you, brethren, to be uninformed of this mystery—so that you will not be wise in your own estimation—that a partial hardening has happened to Israel until the fullness of the Gentiles has come in; **26** and so all Israel will be saved; just as it is written,

"THE DELIVERER WILL COME FROM ZION,
HE WILL REMOVE UNGODLINESS FROM JACOB."
27 "THIS IS MY COVENANT WITH THEM,
WHEN I TAKE AWAY THEIR SINS." *(Isaiah 59:20, 21)*

28 From the standpoint of the gospel they are enemies for your sake, but from the standpoint of *God's* choice they are beloved for the sake of the fathers; **29** for the gifts and the calling of God are irrevocable. **30** For just as you once were disobedient to God, but now have been shown mercy because of their disobedience, **31** so these also now have been disobedient, that because of the mercy shown to you they also may now be shown mercy. **32** For God has shut up all in disobedience so that He may show mercy to all.

THE FULLNESS OF THE GENTILES

25 For I do not want you, brethren, to be uninformed of this mystery—so that you will not be wise in your own estimation—that a partial hardening has happened to Israel until the fullness of the Gentiles has come in;

The "fullness of the Gentiles" is a reference to those Gentiles who will be saved. When the last Gentile is saved, the full number of saved Gentiles will be complete. Remember our description of the word "*plērōma*" in **Verse 12**? Here again, we see a great day coming when all of God's children will be safely home. When the last one has come in, the end of this age will come.

THE BLINDNESS IN PART OF ISRAEL

The God who called out Israel as a special nation has never stopped loving them, even though many were not faithful to Him. Blindness, in part, has come to them. God still has a plan for that remnant who have not forgotten the Lord. They are the true Israel. Even though they are but a small portion of the total nation, they are seen as Israel. Many people today attend churches but are not born again. Just because they align with a particular group does not mean they are true believers.

ALL ISRAEL WILL BE SAVED – WHAT DOES THAT MEAN?

26 and so all Israel will be saved; just as it is written,

"The Deliverer will come from Zion,
He will remove ungodliness from Jacob."
27 "This is My covenant with them
When I take away their sins."

We have seen the remnant of Israel in focus throughout Romans and in the writings of the Prophets, most prominently Isaiah. The presence of a believing remnant is seen in the first verse of this chapter where we read, "I say then, God has not rejected His people, has He? May it never be!"

Who are God's people? Those that are circumcised in heart, not just in the flesh. Those that are children of Abraham by faith, not just ones who cling to family genealogy. These are the ones who have been born of God, not of blood, the will of the flesh, or of man. They are part of the living root of Abraham, Isaac, and Jacob. They are part of the original lump of sanctified dough, the people of faith that have remained true to God over the centuries. They are the remnant, the believing portion of the people of Israel. They are God's people. This is the Israel God is addressing.

God refers to this believing group within the nation of Israel when He says that the hardening of Israel was not complete but only partial. Not all have become hardened. **Verse 25** tells us that God kept a believing remnant, which will be revealed when the believers from the Gentile nations have all come into the fold. The body of Christ will be complete. All true Israel will be saved fulfilling Old Testament prophecies.

This Old Testament quotation is a combination of **Isaiah 59:20, 21** and the New Covenant promise from Jeremiah.

> **"A Redeemer will come to Zion,**
> **And to those who turn from transgression in Jacob," de-**
> **clares the Lord."** (Isaiah 59:20)

> [31] "Behold, days are coming," declares the Lord, "WHEN I WILL MAKE A NEW COVENANT WITH THE HOUSE OF ISRAEL AND WITH THE HOUSE OF JUDAH, [32] not like the covenant which I made with their fathers in the day I took them by the hand to bring them out of the land of Egypt, My covenant which they broke, although I was a husband to them," declares the Lord. [33] "But this is the covenant which I will make with the house of Israel after those days," declares the Lord, "I WILL PUT MY LAW WITHIN THEM AND ON THEIR HEART, I WILL WRITE IT, AND I WILL BE THEIR GOD, AND THEY SHALL BE MY PEOPLE. [34] They will not teach again, each man his neighbor and each man his brother, saying, 'Know the Lord,' FOR THEY WILL ALL KNOW ME, FROM THE LEAST OF THEM TO THE GREATEST OF THEM," DECLARES THE LORD, "FOR I WILL FORGIVE THEIR INIQUITY, AND THEIR SIN I WILL REMEMBER NO MORE." (Jeremiah 31:31-34)

Romans 11 looks forward to that day when these prophecies will be fulfilled. **Verses 29-32** are a strong reminder of the sovereignty of God in the affairs of the Jewish nation and the Gentile peoples of the world. **Verse 29** reminds them and us that when God makes a promise, it is a certainty. His Word is settled in all eternity.

Verses 30 through 32 are all about mercy. We all deserve the holy justice of God but because of the death and resurrection of Christ, God is able to extend mercy to each of us, no matter how grievous our sins. After this glorious promise for both Jew and Gentile, the only thing left is to praise God for His love, goodness, sovereignty, eternal greatness, and mercy. That is what the final four verses say in **Romans 11**.

Paul's hymn of praise to our unfathomable God (11:33-36)

33 Oh, the depth of the riches both of the wisdom and knowledge of God! How unsearchable are His judgments and unfathomable His ways! **34** For WHO HAS KNOWN THE MIND OF THE LORD, OR WHO BECAME HIS COUNSELOR? **35** Or WHO HAS FIRST GIVEN TO HIM THAT IT MIGHT BE PAID BACK TO HIM AGAIN? **36** For from Him and through Him and to Him are all things. To Him *be* the glory forever. Amen.

We have seen the sin of man, the justification of the unjust, the grace of God to all who call on Him, God's faithfulness, sovereignty, love, and grace. Then we saw how He has kept and will keep all His promises to His backslidden people. He used the disobedience of His people Israel for the good of mankind by inviting the Gentile nations into the wedding feast of His Son. After all this, we can only pray the following:

> [33] **"Oh, the depth of the riches both of the wisdom and knowledge of God! How unsearchable are His judgments and unfathomable His ways!"**

What a journey it has been to travel through **Romans 9-11**. Paul lays out an immense presentation to the nation of Israel. He answers all their complaints and concerns, even the charges they had against God. He appeals for His people to return to their God. He promises great hope for all who will come back home into the merciful arms of their Creator. It has been a loving but firm appeal.

At the same time, there was a clear warning to the Gentiles, who have benefited from the hardness of Israel. The warning is not to be arrogant. No man is better than another. Each need to humbly understand that all salvation and blessing finds its roots in God, not man. God alone is sovereign, and yet at the same time, each man is responsible for his own actions. The breadth, scope, and hope, found in these three chapters are breathtaking. How can we mortals even begin to comprehend the mind and ways of God?

34 "For who has known the mind of the Lord, or who became His counselor? **35** Or who has first given to Him that it might be paid back to him again?"

Paul concludes the three chapters with a hymn of praise, a doxology, a song from his heart. Through it all, Paul seems to be overwhelmed by the infinite attributes of God; wisdom, knowledge, holy justice, His will and His heart. He is unsearchable and unfathomable. He is the God of Israel. He is the God of the nations. He is Paul's God. He is our God. Everything is for His glory. Amen and amen!

36 For **from** Him and **through** Him and **to** Him are all things. To Him *be* the glory forever. Amen.

LOOKING AHEAD TO ROMANS CHAPTERS 12-16

The first eleven chapters led us from sin to salvation to sanctification. They were doctrinal in nature. The final five chapters will show us ways to serve God and man. Now that we are Christians, we will see how we are to live our Christian lives in a broken world.

The last five chapters are about practical Christian living.

"Oh, the depth of the riches both of the wisdom and knowledge of God! How unsearchable are His judgments and unfathomable His ways! "

Romans 11:33

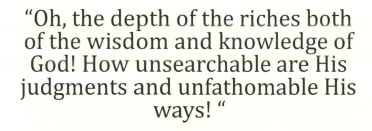

 **GENTILES**   **ISRAEL**

Romans Chapter 12

Living out our Christian lives in an ungodly world

CHAPTER OVERVIEW

After laying out a strong foundation for our journey from sin to salvation, Paul now begins a new section of his Epistle. **Chapter 12** is the beginning of instructions about how we are to live as Christians in an ungodly world. He begins with a strong appeal for each of us to be fully consecrated to God. We are to lay our lives on God's altar of spiritual sacrifice. After all, Jesus laid it all on the cross for us. He reminds us just how special and gifted by God we are. The proper attitudes we need to be effective in using the gifts God has given to us. He finishes this chapter appealing to the believers to be genuinely devoted to each other, he gives instructions on how to deal with people that hurt us.

THE KEY VERSES FOR CHAPTER 12

[1]"Therefore I urge you, brethren, by the mercies of God, to present your bodies a living and holy sacrifice, acceptable to God, which is your spiritual service of worship. [2] And do not be conformed to this world, but be transformed by the renewing of your mind, so that you may prove what the will of God is, that which is good and acceptable and perfect."

SIMPLE OUTLINE

I. Romans 12:1-2 - Fully surrendered to God.

II. Romans 12:3-8 - Each believer has a unique gift and purpose.

III. Romans 12:9-13 - Devoted to one another.

IV. Romans 12:14-21 - How to deal with people that hurt us.

Romans 12 Commentary

Romans 12:1-2. Fully surrendered to God

1 Therefore I urge you, brethren, by the mercies of God, to present your bodies a living and holy sacrifice, acceptable to God, *which is* your spiritual service of worship. **2** And do not be conformed to this world, but be transformed by the renewing of your mind, so that you may prove what the will of God is, that which is good and acceptable and perfect.

This new section of **Romans** is about how Christians should live. **Verses 1 and 2** lay the critical foundation to ensure the house stands. That strong foundation is a heart for God, completely dedicated to Him. The Roman environment was tough, not a place for the weak. Jesus talked about the foolishness of building a house on sand. If a heart is committed to God, then no matter what comes, the house stands. The Church stands because it is built on the Rock, Jesus Christ.

1 Therefore I urge you, brethren, by the mercies of God, to present your bodies a living and holy sacrifice, acceptable to God, *which is* your spiritual service of worship.

The Old Testament sacrificial system is clearly pictured in this verse. There were two classes of sacrifices listed in **Leviticus 1-7**. Every Jew and many Gentiles were familiar with these. There were mandatory sacrifices which dealt with forgiveness of sin. The second category concerned worship, consecration, fellowship, and thanksgiving. These were optional for those whose sins were forgiven. Whether for sin or for the purpose of worship, all offerings were to be the best. A spotless lamb, the finest flour, always the best. We are exhorted in **Verse one** to present ourselves to God in a "holy and acceptable" way. God sent His best for us, and we should do no less for God.

We as children of God, worship and praise God. We show our thanksgiving to our Savior and King by dedicating our lives to the One who gave it all on the cross for us. He laid down His life so we can live. We are asked to do the reasonable thing. Give our lives to serve our glorious Savior and King. Nothing held back. This is true worship. We cannot live a successful Christian life without being fully committed to God.

2 And do not be conformed to this world, but be transformed by the renewing of your mind, so that you may prove what the will of God is, that which is good and acceptable and perfect.

The literal Greek meaning of the opening command is "And (you are) to stop conforming yourselves to this age." The lost are on a destructive path that leads to a horrible eternity. No believer should live his life in the same way as the lost live.

This verse presents two paths. The first leads to disaster. It is never God's will to conform to the thinking and practice of the lost. When we allow God to begin the process of changing us into the image of His Son, the result, according to this verse, is good and acceptable and perfect. Jesus said it would not be easy.

> **"If you were of the world, the world would love its own; but because you are not of the world, but I chose you out of the world, therefore the world hates you."** (John 15:19)

James adds to that warning:

> **"You adulteresses, do you not know that friendship with the world is hostility toward God? Therefore, whoever wishes to be a friend of the world makes himself an enemy of God."** (James 4:4)

When we consider these first two verses together, we see there is something we are to do and something we are to avoid. We are to fully surrender to God. We are to avoid the ways of the lost age in which we live. All Christian living begins here.

In **Verses 3-8,** we see just how special and gifted we are.

SPIRITUAL GIFTS

What are Spiritual Gifts? Think of a homeowner that has different appliances in the kitchen. The stove is for cooking, the toaster is for toasting bread, the blender is for mixing and the refrigerator makes ice. Each has a different purpose and should be used the way they were designed, Likewise, each believer has an assigned place in the function of the Church. He has been given the capacity to do exactly what he is called upon to do. The Holy Spirit is the power source. We need to make the connection, so we can do what we are designed to do. The sad thing in many churches is that many believers never realize what they could do. Many gifts remain dormant, unconnected to the Spirit of God. He alone can energize the potential God has built into us.

What are the different Spiritual Gifts? Four Bible passages tell us.

- **Ephesians 4:12**. Ephesians lists four types of gifted people that God uses to establish and grow churches. These are the Apostles, Prophets, Evangelists, and the Pastor/Teacher. These gifts can be looked at as church establishment, or foundation-laying gifts.

- **1 Peter 4:10-11.** Peter reminds the church that God has given certain gifts that involve speaking and serving. We are to use them to glorify God.

- **1 Corinthians 12:4-11, 28.** Paul lists a wide variety of gifts God has given to build the body of Christ. He is clear that no gift is for personal gain but for the common good of the Church. Eleven gifts are listed and range from teaching and communicating to serving, helping, administering and also signs and wonders. These are sometimes referred to as ministry gifts.

- **Romans 12:6-8.** A shorter but similar list as **1 Corinthians**. The focus is on how each gifted member of the church is to use their gifts with diligence and joy. When we do, we support the leadership and outreach of the church and bring glory to God.

- **Old Testament passages** also reveal that God has given other special enablings of the Spirit for specific purposes. These include, but are not limited to, music, the arts, and fine craftsmanship that God gave for the building of the Tabernacle. **(Exodus 35:10-19)**

Romans 12:3-8. Each believer has a unique Spiritual gift and purpose

3 For through the grace given to me I say to everyone among you not to think more highly of himself than he ought to think; but to think so as to have sound judgment, as God has allotted to each a measure of faith. **4** For just as we have many members in one body and all the members do not have the same function, **5** so we, who are many, are one body in Christ, and individually members one of another. **6** Since we have gifts that differ according to the grace given to us, *each of us is to exercise them accordingly*: if prophecy, according to the proportion of his faith; **7** if service, in his serving; or he who teaches, in his teaching; **8** or he who exhorts, in his exhortation; he who gives, with liberality; he who leads, with diligence; he who shows mercy, with cheerfulness.

As we have seen, there are four passages in the New Testament that deal with Spiritual Gifts. The Ephesian passage describes four different gifted people that God has assigned to establish, defend, grow and advance the Church. These are the Apostles, Prophets, Evangelists and the Pastor/Teacher. Peter reminds us that the gifts are to be used to serve the Church and glorify God. They are not for our benefit, but for the body of Christ. Paul, in **1 Corinthians 12-14,** teaches the same thing, the gifts are for the common good, not for personal edification.

The list in **1 Corinthians** is the most exhaustive and is quite similar to the list we find in **Romans 12**, which is slightly smaller. Paul wrote both Epistles, but to different audiences.

The Corinthian letter was primarily written to address sins and abuses found in the church. In that letter, Paul handles misunderstandings about what the gifts are, how they are to be used and rebukes believers for their selfish abuses of the gifts God has given them.

Romans 12 has a unique tone to it. He reminds them that gifts come from God, there is nothing to boast in, since they come from God. They are gifts of grace, totally undeserved. Paul emphasizes that this attitude is to be what defines the church at Rome.

UNITY AND DIVERSITY

3 For through the grace given to me I say to everyone among you not to think more highly of himself than he ought to think; but to think so as to have sound judgment, as God has allotted to each a measure of faith. **4** For just as we have many members in one body and all the members do not have the same function, **5** so we, who are many, are one body in Christ, and individually members one of another.

Gifts come from God. We don't take credit for them. They are each unique, since we are each unique. We recognize that God has assigned the gifts. We should be unified with thankful hearts for our differences. Unity and diversity are what makes us a special community. We need God, and we need one another.

"I can do all things through Him who strengthens me." (Philippians 4:13)

"I am the vine, you are the branches; he who abides in Me and I in him, he bears much fruit, for apart from Me you can do nothing." (John 15:5)

Everything we do, every skill and position we hold, should honor God. If our attitudes are humble, as they should be, then we will be unified in Christ. We will together glorify Him.

GOD'S MEASURING CUP

"As God has allotted to each a measure of faith."

We measure things every day in our lives. We measure our ingredients to put in the food we prepare. We measure out distances, volumes or available space. We wouldn't want to pour a gallon of water into a small glass. Did you ever think that God knows us completely? He understands our capacity and exactly what we can handle. He carefully measures out just how many trials we can handle, how much heat we can endure. He knows our individual strengths and weaknesses. When He distributes spiritual gifts, He knows exactly what we can use and what is best for us, and what is best for the body of Christ.

It is not just an amount of faith that He gives us, it is His exact amount of faith that He has measured out to give us. It is perfect.

EACH OF US IS GIVEN AN ASSIGNMENT IN THE BODY OF CHRIST

6 Since we have gifts that differ according to the grace given to us, *each of us is to exercise them accordingly*: if prophecy, according to the proportion of his faith; **7** if service, in his serving; or he who teaches, in his teaching; **8** or he who exhorts, in his exhortation; he who gives, with liberality; he who leads, with diligence; he who shows mercy, with cheerfulness.

The primary focus and difference between **Romans** and **1 Corinthians** is the purpose of writing about the gifts. Paul wrote to the church in Corinth to correct a series of abuses and sins found in the church. The people were using the gifts of God for personal edification and selfish purposes. Paul makes clear in that letter that the gifts are for the body and every member of the body. The gifts they have been given are equally important.

Unlike **1 Corinthians**, **Romans 12** is not trying to prevent abuses, but is promoting the uses of the gifts. The new element found in Romans is the attitude of the one exercising the gifts. If giving, then it is to be done generously. If leading, it should be done with diligence. The one that shows mercy should do it cheerfully. All the gifts need to be exercised with grace to others recognizing that the gifts are themselves gifts of grace to us from God. We need to keep that attitude when we use them.

The big message is God has given you a custom designed gift package, and you need to use it. Keep a humble spirit and boast only in God. We have been blessed with the great privilege of serving.

What will a church look like when its members actually do that? The next passage, **Romans 12:9-13**, gives us a glimpse of that kind of church.

Romans 12:9-13. Devoted to one another

9 *Let* love *be* without hypocrisy. Abhor what is evil; cling to what is good. **10** *Be* devoted to one another in brotherly love; give preference to one another in honor; **11** not lagging behind in diligence, fervent in spirit, serving the Lord; **12** rejoicing in hope, persevering in tribulation, devoted to prayer, **13** contributing to the needs of the saints, practicing hospitality.

THE IDEAL CHURCH

Think about what we have learned so far in **Romans 12:1-8**. For the church to be the church that honors God and functions the way He intended, each believer must fully dedicate himself to God and let God transform him and renew his mind. Each believer needs to thank God for the special gifting he has been given, and by faith, accept his role in the body of Christ. Each believer should serve the Church with joy, and use their gifts for others in the body.

Imagine what the Church would be like if every believer lived out **Verses 9-13**. The following list is what others would see when they look at that Church:

The believers ...

- Deeply love one another.

- Never have any motive for their actions but to help each other.

- Turn away from evil acts or intentions.

- Only pursue those things that do well for others.

- Want to serve others instead of themselves.

- Rejoice in their trials and endure their hardships with grace.

- Are strong in prayer every day.

- Are generous and joyful in giving of their time, talents and treasure.

To summarize. If a church existed that did nothing else but believe and follow the instructions given in these five verses, we would have a church that never had a church fight, never lacked finances, were continually bringing people to Christ, were joyful, were encouraged and looked for ways to encourage others. They would serve without asking, never complain about any trial, would pray for each other and their pastor all the time and have their homes and lives open to the needy around them. They would impact the entire community around them. Does this describe your church? Maybe we need to spend more time in **Romans 12:9-13**. It begins with leadership who model it.

But what do we do when others don't seek to live by these instructions? **How do we handle those who try to hurt us, or do evil things against us?**

That leads to **Romans 12:14-21**.

Romans 12:14-21. Dealing with people that hurt us.

14 Bless those who persecute you; bless and do not curse. **15** Rejoice with those who rejoice, and weep with those who weep. **16** Be of the same mind toward one another; do not be haughty in mind, but associate with the lowly. Do not be wise in your own estimation. **17** Never pay back evil for evil to anyone. Respect what is right in the sight of all men. **18** If possible, so far as it depends on you, be at peace with all men. **19** Never take your own revenge, beloved, but leave room for the wrath *of God*, for it is written, "Vengeance is Mine, I will repay," says the Lord. **20** "But if your enemy is hungry, feed him, and if he is thirsty, give him a drink; for in so doing you will heap burning coals on his head." **21** Do not be overcome by evil, but overcome evil with good.

Nobody likes persecution. We want people to like us, not curse us. However, it is not a perfect world, is it? We saw in the previous verses what an ideal church might look like, even in an imperfect world. Now, we look at how we, as believers, deal with that imperfect world when it shows its fangs and strikes like a poisonous snake. Sometimes, the attacks come from within the body of Christ. Someone has said that the church is the only army that shoots its wounded. Members of the church can sometimes really hurt one another. What should we do when that happens?

Before we briefly examine how to handle difficulties, it is helpful to see how Jesus handled them.

> **"Although He was a Son, He learned obedience from the things which He suffered".** (Hebrews 5:8)

"Blessed are you when people insult you and persecute you, and falsely say all kinds of evil against you because of Me. [12] Rejoice and be glad, for your reward in heaven is great; for in the same way they persecuted the prophets who were before you." (Matthew 5:11-12)

"He was oppressed and He was afflicted,
Yet He did not open His mouth;
Like a lamb that is led to slaughter,
And like a sheep that is silent before its shearers,
So He did not open His mouth." (Isaiah 53:7)

"If the world hates you, you know that it has hated Me before it hated you. [19] If you were of the world, the world would love its own; but because you are not of the world, but I chose you out of the world, because of this the world hates you." (John 15:18. 19)

There are many more Scriptures concerning suffering and persecution. We are in the world and will have persecution. What sets us apart from the world is how we respond to persecution and the trials we face as believers. Let's look briefly at several issues of life that Paul addresses. They are issues that we need to respond to in a Biblical fashion.

14 Bless those who persecute you; bless and do not curse.

In **1 Peter 4:12** we are reminded, *"Beloved, do not be surprised at the fiery ordeal among you, which comes upon you for your testing, as though some strange thing were happening to you."* It is going to happen, we already know. There is nothing to shock us. The world does not handle persecution well, they curse at it, they defend themselves, they retaliate and get even. We are not like that, at least we shouldn't be. With God's help, we can actually treat our attackers with grace. We understand they are being led by their sin nature. They hate us because they hate Jesus. With God's help, we can help them by blessing them, showing kindness to them and not responding the way they expect us to respond, by cursing them. They will see Jesus in us.

15 Rejoice with those who rejoice, and weep with those who weep.

Solomon wrote that there were seasons for everything;

> **"A time to weep and a time to laugh;**
> **A time to mourn and a time to dance"** (Ecclesiastes 3:4)

This verse describes times like this. All people in the world have to deal with loss, that includes believers. We don't grieve like those who don't have eternal hope. We carry something with us that unbelievers don't carry. We have the love of Jesus. We are emotional beings, and God can use all emotions for good. We should radiate the love of Christ in every circumstance, the good along with the difficult.

16 Be of the same mind toward one another; do not be haughty in mind, but associate with the lowly. Do not be wise in your own estimation.

Prejudice is like poison. It kills everything it touches. It breaks apart relationships, ruins our testimony, hurts those around us, and it will tear our ministry and church apart. We need to remind ourselves again and again that it was all because of God's grace that we are children of God. *"For I know that good itself does not dwell in me, that is, in my sinful nature."* (**Romans 7:18**).

Paul makes it practical and tells the believers in Rome to associate with the lowly, the ones they formerly thought were below them. Associate with those who can't pay you back. Show compassion on the poor and never look at them as less than yourself. This thinking is radical thinking to a world that looks at people like stepping stones to success. The Christian should want to bless and help those that others just want to use.

17 Never pay back evil for evil to anyone. Respect what is right in the sight of all men. **18** If possible, so far as it depends on you, be at peace with all men. **19** Never take your own revenge, beloved, but leave room for the wrath *of God*, for it is written, "VENGEANCE IS MINE, I WILL REPAY," says the Lord.

"**Blessed are the peacemakers: for they shall be called the children of God.** (Matthew 5:9)

"**You have heard that it was said, 'An eye for an eye, and a tooth for a tooth.'** [39] **But I say to you, do not resist an evil person; but whoever slaps you on your right cheek, turn the other to him also.** [40] **If anyone wants to sue you and take your shirt, let him have your coat also.** [41] **Whoever forces you to go one mile, go with him two.** [42] **Give to him who asks of you, and do not turn away from him who wants to borrow from you.** (Matthew 5:38-42)

Jesus always stunned the crowds and the religious leaders of His time with words like these. He spoke with authority, not like the teachers of His day. His words came from a different kingdom, and do not resemble the wisdom of this lost world. **Romans 12:17-19** sounds like it could have easily been a part of the Sermon on the Mount. They are not the ways of the world, but counsel from Heaven, given by the One who knows human nature better than we do. He alone knows how to bring peace to a volatile situation. He alone can calm the savage beast of man's heart that cries out for vengeance and war when attacked. We need to listen to the voice of reason and calm, the only voice that can be trusted when dark emotions rise up within us. There is a calm peace in God's presence and when we spend time with Him. That is the air we are breathing.

Then we are ready to respond, but not the way our attackers respond. They do evil, but we do not have to act that way towards them. It is when we respond this way that the world takes notice. It is then that they see Jesus in us. The worst of times can become the best of times.

20 "But if your enemy is hungry, feed him, and if he is thirsty, give him a drink; for in so doing you will heap burning coals on his head." **21** Do not be overcome by evil, but overcome evil with good.

WHAT ARE THOSE BURNING COALS?

The passage is quoted from Proverbs 25:21-22

> "If your enemy is hungry, give him food to eat;
> And if he is thirsty, give him water to drink;
> ²² For you will heap burning coals on his head,
> And the Lord will reward you."

Paul is quoting an ancient idiom that was referenced by Solomon. There is no explanation given. We can assume it was an idiom that the people must have understood in their time, even if we don't use it today.

Historians, theologians, and archaeologists have tried to find the meaning, but we can't be totally sure today. There is one particular ancient writing which may give some hint as to the usage of that idiom. It comes from a book most Christians have never read. It is one of the Apocryphal books found in some Bibles. The Apocryphal books are viewed by evangelicals as a useful history, but not inspired text. There are many useful historical documents that we have today. Students use them to unearth information about ancient cultures. They can be very helpful at times. It does not mean they have inspired Scripture, just ancient history. The books of **Esdras** and **2 Esdras** (thought to be written by Ezra) are examples of history found in the Catholic Bible and Eastern Orthodox and Ethiopian Bibles that may provide a helpful window of understanding into this ancient idiom of putting hot coals on someone's head.

> **2 Esdras 16:53, 64-65 (I King James Version)**
> **53** "Let not the sinner say that he hath not sinned: for God shall burn coals of fire upon his head, which saith before the Lord God and his glory, I have not sinned.
>
> **64** Therefore hath the Lord exactly searched out all your works, and he will put you all to shame.
> **65** And when your sins are brought forth, ye shall be ashamed before men, and your own sins shall be your accusers in that day."

Paul and Solomon apparently were describing the shame a person feels. When a person realized he was a sinner or his sin was exposed before men, it was a great embarrassment. It felt like hot coals were burning into his head. When a Christian shows love to his enemies, and feeds his accusers, it reveals their dark motives and makes them feel ashamed. They feel like hot coals are on their head. It is a description of deep shame when good overcomes evil **(Verse 21)**. The end result is that God gets Glory. That is the goal of all these instructions and should be the goal of all we do as Christians.

Loving and serving one another is a continuing theme in the next chapters. First, Paul has an important issue to discuss. **How is a Christian to respond to a corrupt and evil government? Should we support it or rebel against it?**

¹⁵ "I have set you an example that you should do as I have done for you. ¹⁶ Very truly I tell you, no servant is greater than his master, nor is a messenger greater than the one who sent him." (John 13:15,16)

Romans Chapter 13
Living out our faith in an ungodly society

CHAPTER OVERVIEW

Paul continues his list of practical instructions to the Romans about how they are to live their daily lives in a non-Christian world. This chapter is unique in Scripture as it contains the only practical instructions about how a Christian is to behave and respond to the government where they live. In this case, to a corrupt and immoral government. The second topic is the importance of loving our neighbor, not just in the church, but all those around us. The third topic is how believers should deal with maintaining their moral purity in an immoral world.

THE KEY VERSES FOR CHAPTER 13

[1]"Every person is to be in subjection to the governing authorities. For there is no authority except from God, and those which exist are established by God. [2] Therefore whoever resists authority has opposed the ordinance of God; and they who have opposed will receive condemnation upon themselves."

SIMPLE OUTLINE

I. Romans 13:1-7 — The Christian and the government.

II. Romans 13:8-10 — A debt of love.

III. Romans 13:11-14 — Importance of moral purity.

Romans 13 Commentary

Romans 13:1-7. The Christian and the government

1Every person is to be in subjection to the governing authorities. For there is no authority except from God, and those which exist are established by God. **2** Therefore whoever resists authority has opposed the ordinance of God; and they who have opposed will receive condemnation upon themselves. **3** For rulers are not a cause of fear for good behavior, but for evil. Do you want to have no fear of authority? Do what is good and you will have praise from the same; **4** for it is a minister of God to you for good. But if you do what is evil, be afraid; for it does not bear the sword for nothing; for it is a minister of God, an avenger who brings wrath on the one who practices evil. **5** Therefore it is necessary to be in subjection, not only because of wrath, but also for conscience' sake. **6** For because of this you also pay taxes, for *rulers* are servants of God, devoting themselves to this very thing. **7** Render to all what is due them: tax to whom tax *is due*; custom to whom custom; fear to whom fear; honor to whom honor.

In **Chapter 12,** we learned that we are expected to fully dedicate our lives to God much like the Burnt Offerings were to be fully consumed as worship. Then, we learned that each member of the body of Christ was to be devoted to one another.

It must have been a difficult conflict for those living under the corrupt and immoral government of Rome and forced to pay taxes and duties to support that government, which was opposed to the Christian message and way of life. They must have struggled with the problem of being loyal to God, and at the same time being asked to be loyal to Caesar by supporting the building of pagan temples. What was a Christian to do?

Paul answers those issues in **Romans 13:1-7.**

WE ARE TO BE GOOD CITIZENS BY OBEYING OUR GOVERNMENT

1Every person is to be in subjection to the governing authorities. For there is no authority except from God, and those which exist are established by God. **2** Therefore whoever resists authority has opposed the ordinance of God; and they who have opposed will receive condemnation upon themselves.

When addressing the issue of loyalty to God or loyalty to country, Paul begins with the same issue he raised in **Chapters 9-11** when answering Israel's complaints against God. Sovereignty. God is ultimately sovereign in every matter. All governments, even the evil ones, are under His divine hand. He is not only fully aware of every aspect of them but for reasons known only to Him, He has actually established them.

The book of **Habakkuk** in the Old Testament tells of the struggle and questions the prophet had with God when He raised up the Babylonians to chastise Israel. In **Habakkuk 1**, he argued back to God that the Lord is too Holy to use the evil Babylonians to chastise His children, Israel. God reminded Habakkuk that He is God. He is sovereign. He raises nations and peoples for His purposes and glory.

God had given Daniel a vision showing each empire He would raise up from Babylon to Persia, to Greece, and, yes, even Rome.

He is God. He is in control. That is why Jesus answered the Pharisees the way He did when He told them:

> **"Then render to Caesar the things that are Caesar's; and to God the things that are God's."** (Matthew 22:22)

Since the government is in the hand of God and established by Him for His ultimate purpose, then for us to rebel against that government is to rebel against God Himself. That is Paul's argument in **Verse 2.** The only exception is when a government demands we violate the Law of God. Then, we take our stand with God. This situation happened in the time of Moses with the midwives and with Daniel when the people were commanded to worship an idol. Here is one instance in **Acts**:

> [27] **"When they had brought them, they stood them before the Council. The high priest questioned them,** [28] **saying, "We gave you strict orders not to continue teaching in this name, and yet, you have filled Jerusalem with your teaching and intend to bring this man's blood upon us."** [29] **But Peter and the apostles answered, "We must obey God rather than men."** (Acts 5:27-29)

THE AUTHORITY OF THE GOVERNMENT

3 For rulers are not a cause of fear for good behavior, but for evil. Do you want to have no fear of authority? Do what is good and you will have praise from the same; **4** for it is a minister of God to you for good. But if you do what is evil, be afraid; for it does not bear the sword for nothing; for it is a minister of God, an avenger who brings wrath on the one who practices evil. **5** Therefore it is necessary to be in subjection, not only because of wrath, but also for conscience' sake.

For the person who lives life obeying the rule of the land, that person has little to fear. The lawbreaker has much to fear.

Since God has established governments, then any rebellion against what God has established is a rebellion against His will — against God Himself. There are consequences to rebellion, and the government is the one assigned to carry out the justice for the rebellious people. They are in essence "an avenger who brings wrath on the one who practices evil." **(Verse 4)**

This brings up the phrase, "for it does not bear the sword for nothing." The sword is the implement used to dispense the ultimate justice of God. The government has been given the right to enforce the death penalty.

CAPITAL PUNISHMENT

God was clear in the Old Testament that man was not to take another person's life. If they did, they would forfeit their own life. It was God's justice. A surgeon removes a cancerous tumor to save the life of a patient. God did the same. He laid down a law to save humanity from moral cancer that would result in self-destruction. This is the first command God gave:

> [6] **"Whoever sheds man's blood, By man his blood shall be shed, For in the image of God He made man.** [7] **"As for you, be fruitful and multiply; Populate the earth abundantly and multiply in it."** (Genesis 9:6, 7)

Capital punishment is not murder. It is God's justice for a murderer. The command was given to the entire human race, not just a select people. The justice was initially carried out in the early years of humanity by each person who had been wronged. By the time of Moses, the same law of justice was expanded and reinforced for the people of God.

> **"Thus, you shall not show pity: life for life, eye for eye, tooth for tooth, hand for hand, foot for foot." (**Deuteronomy 19:21**)**

Some confuse what Jesus later said and think He removed capital punishment.

> [38] **"You have heard that it was said, 'AN EYE FOR AN EYE, AND A TOOTH FOR A TOOTH.'** [39] **But I say to you, do not resist an evil person; but whoever slaps you on your right cheek, turn the other to him also." (**Matthew 5:38, 39)

What changed was not capital punishment, the justice of God, but how it was administered. Before there were governments, each person handled the matter personally. Jesus was telling the people that, individually, they no longer had the role of dispensing God's justice against the murderer. This was now the Government's responsibility. Their role was to let the government do their part. Their job was to forgive the offender. This is reaffirmed by Paul in **Romans 13**. The Roman government is the one who punishes the offender and executes capital punishment by the sword. They are now God's assigned avenger against the offender.

One final note. Some today say that capital punishment is not a deterrent to further crime. That is wrong for several reasons. First, it is still the moral Law of God and has not been taken away by God. Second, the main reason for the

Law was not just to be a deterrent but to show man how serious God is about murder. Third, because today it isn't done quickly, people think they will one day get away with the crime. Finally, they can never murder again.

[11] "Because the sentence against an evil deed is not executed quickly, therefore the hearts of the sons of men among them are given fully to do evil." (Ecclesiastes 8:11)

A TAXING PROBLEM

6 For because of this you also pay taxes, for rulers are servants of God, devoting themselves to this very thing. **7** Render to all what is due them: tax to whom tax is due; custom to whom custom; fear to whom fear; honor to whom honor.

Someone will ask, "Why should I pay taxes to a government to support things I don't think are right? For example, should a Christian pay taxes to a government that supports abortion? Yes, you should pay your taxes to your government, even when you can't agree with how they use them. You are not condoning these things. The government is doing that. Jesus paid taxes to Rome, a government that promoted temple prostitutes, built new pagan temples for worship, and supplied them with idols from taxes they collected from people that opposed idolatry.

Taxes are the rent we pay to live in a certain country for the privilege to accomplish God's Kingdom ministry. It is the same as when a renter pays his landlord, even when his landlord is ungodly. Jesus paid His taxes, and even called a tax collector, Matthew, to be one of His disciples. The bottom line is we owe an allegiance to the government, unless we are commanded to violate the Law of God. The next verses talk about another debt, the debt of love we owe to each other.

Romans 13:8-10. We owe a debt of love

8 Owe nothing to anyone except to love one another; for he who loves his neighbor has fulfilled *the* law. **9** For this, "YOU SHALL NOT COMMIT ADULTERY, YOU SHALL NOT MURDER, YOU SHALL NOT STEAL, YOU SHALL NOT COVET," AND IF THERE IS ANY OTHER COMMANDMENT, IT IS SUMMED UP IN THIS SAYING, "YOU SHALL LOVE YOUR NEIGHBOR AS YOURSELF." **10** Love does no wrong to a neighbor; therefore, love is the fulfillment of *the* law.

There are different kinds of debt. Financial debt is when we owe money to someone. It could be for a variety of reasons. Financial debt is a form of slavery according to Proverbs.

There is also a spiritual debt. We are always in debt to God for what He has done to purchase our salvation. We can't begin to pay Him back. We can honor God by obeying Him and loving Him by loving His Church. We express that love by doing nothing that harms others in any way **(Verse 10).**

The rich young ruler **(Mark 10:17-27)** learned how hard it was to love his neighbor as himself. We honor God when we seek His help to do that. It is actually a privilege to have this debt with God and man. It means we have been purchased from the depths of sin and lifted into the light. At one point, we were under the crushing burden and penalty of our sin. The wages of sin is death, and that was our deserved sentence. We owed a debt we could not pay. God paid a debt He didn't owe. Now we are free from the penalty of sin. It is a great privilege to be a bondslave of God, a debtor to His grace forever. Part of that debt of love is to love others.

The final challenge in this chapter is to recognize the lateness of the hour and not waste our lives by using them for fleshly pursuits.

Romans 13:11-14. The importance of moral purity

11 *Do* this, knowing the time, that it is already the hour for you to awaken from sleep; for now, salvation is nearer to us than when we believed. **12** The night is almost gone, and the day is near. Therefore, let us lay aside the deeds of darkness and put on the armor of light. **13** Let us behave properly as in the day, not in carousing and drunkenness, not in sexual promiscuity and sensuality, not in strife and jealousy. **14** But put on the Lord Jesus Christ, and make no provision for the flesh in regard to *its* lusts.

Verse 11 may sound confusing, "salvation is nearer to us than when we believed." Salvation in Scripture is described in the past tense at times, present tense at times and in this verse in a future tense. It is a grand word that covers everything from the time we were saved to the time we will be with God in eternity. When we trusted Christ, we were saved from the penalty of sin. That is past tense.

As we learned in **Romans 7**, we still struggle with our flesh. The good news is that the power of the Holy Spirit can keep us from submitting to the daily temptations of sin in our fallen flesh, which wars with our spirit. We can be delivered daily from the power of sin. That is the present state of salvation.

One day, in Glory, when the curse is over, and we are with the Lord, we will be delivered from the very presence of sin forever. **Salvation affects the penalty of sin (past), the power of sin, (present) and presence of sin (future tense of salvation).**

Imagine taking a railroad journey. Your ticket is purchased. You board the train. The track leads to your destination. Along the way, you encounter storms and threatening events, but you are kept on the track. One day you finally arrive at your destination.

This passage is saying your final destination is just ahead, it is nearer than when you first got on the train. What a great hope!

The cry of this verse is for Christians to "Wake up! Don't you know how late it is?" That Great Day is approaching quickly. There are still many people that need to know Christ.

12 The night is almost gone, and the day is near. Therefore, let us lay aside the deeds of darkness and put on the armor of light.

Since that Great Day is coming soon when we will be with Jesus and all our work on earth is done, we need to be diligent to redeem the time. We only have these precious few moments to do our Father's work. The night is almost over, the Great Day of the Lord approaches.

> **"We must work the works of Him who sent Me as long as it is day; night is coming when no one can work."** (John 9:4)

> **"Therefore be careful how you walk, not as unwise men but as wise, [16] making the most of your time, because the days are evil. [17] So then do not be foolish, but understand what the will of the Lord is."** (Ephesians 5:15-17)

If we are to use our time well for the Kingdom of God, then we need to be careful about wasting time. Time is a precious thing. The deeds of darkness have infiltrated the Church. Many believers have become too friendly with the damaging ways of the lost world. It must have been like that in the Roman empire. Paul warns the believers, **"let us lay aside the deeds of darkness and put on the armor of light."** His command is very relevant today. **"The night is almost gone, and the day is near."**

13 Let us behave properly as in the day, not in carousing and drunkenness, not in sexual promiscuity and sensuality, not in strife and jealousy. **14** But put on the Lord Jesus Christ, and make no provision for the flesh in regard to its lusts.

Paul closes out his warnings and exhortations in this chapter with a warning specifically targeting the dangers and the allurements of sins of the flesh. He specifically lists sins that were rampant in the first century Rome, where the pursuit of pleasure was like a national sport. His list includes:

- **Carousing, or partying**
- **Drunkenness**
- **Sexual promiscuity**
- **Sensuality**
- **Strife**
- **Jealousy**

As we see these things increasing today, we also see increased suicide rate among young people, widespread drug usage and depression, resulting in people devoid of joy and healthy emotions. The pursuit of pleasure was widespread then and it is increasing today.

> **"But immorality or any impurity or greed must not even be named among you, as is proper among saints;"**
> (Ephesians 5:3)

Brothers and sisters, we who claim Christ have no time for this. The daylight is soon coming, the night is ending. We are children of God. The world is looking for Jesus but they don't know it. They are looking for hope, but in the wrong places. They want joy, but where will they find it? They will one day look at you and me. What will they see?

Romans Chapter 14
Judging each other, stumbling blocks and personal conscience issues

Therefore let us not judge one another anymore, but rather determine this—not to put an obstacle or a stumbling block in a brother's way

(Romans 14:13)

CHAPTER OVERVIEW

Chapter 14 focuses on various aspects of how Christians judge and hurt other Christians. It may be because a weaker brother is not strong enough to understand the freedom he has in Christ concerning certain foods or religious practices. Some Christians condemn other believers because they don't worship or act like they do. Paul warns that one day we all will stand before the judgment seat of Christ and give an account of the ways we hurt one another. He concludes with a strong warning about putting any kind of stumbling block in front of another believer. Tolerance of one another in the body of Christ is the goal of the Chapter.

THE KEY VERSES FOR CHAPTER 14

[21] **"It is good not to eat meat or to drink wine, or to do anything by which your brother stumbles.** [22] **The faith which you have, have as your own conviction before God. Happy is he who does not condemn himself in what he approves.** [23] **But he who doubts is condemned if he eats, because his eating is not from faith; and whatever is not from faith is sin."**

SIMPLE OUTLINE

Romans 14:1-4 — We are not to judge others in regards to food.

Romans 14:5-9 — We are not to judge others in regards to religious practices.

Romans 14:10-12 — All of our actions against our brethren will be judged by God.

Romans 14:13-23 — We are not to do anything that causes a believer to stumble.

Romans 14 Commentary

Romans 14:1-4 We are not to judge others in regards to food.

1Now accept the one who is weak in faith, *but* not for *the purpose of* passing judgment on his opinions. **2** One person has faith that he may eat all things, but he who is weak eats vegetables *only*. **3** The one who eats is not to regard with contempt the one who does not eat, and the one who does not eat is not to judge the one who eats, for God has accepted him. **4** Who are you to judge the servant of another? To his own master he stands or falls; and he will stand, for the Lord is able to make him stand.

Remember when Peter denied knowing Jesus three times? Peter knew he had done a horrible thing. He wept bitterly. After the resurrection, Jesus gave Peter an opportunity to begin again. He asked him three times if he really loved Him.

> **"Peter was grieved because He said to him the third time, "Do you love Me?" And he said to Him, "Lord, You know all things; You know that I love You." Jesus *said to him, "Tend My sheep."** (John 21:17)

Jesus was giving Peter another chance to make right what he had done. He denied Christ three times. He told Jesus he loved Him three times. You would think that the joy of being put back into a right and loving relationship would be enough. It is interesting to see what happened next.

> [20] **"Peter, turning around, saw the disciple whom Jesus loved following them; the one who also had leaned back on His bosom at the supper and said, "Lord, who is the one**

who betrays You?" [21] So Peter seeing him *said to Jesus, "Lord, and what about this man?" [22] Jesus *said to him, "If I want him to remain until I come, what is that to you? You follow Me!" (John 21:20-22)

Instead of praising Jesus for being forgiven, Peter sees John and asks Jesus, "What about this guy? What is going to happen to him? Jesus' answer was simple, "What is that to you?"

In other words, we have no business pointing out another's faults, their lives, or their choices. God will take care of them. He is dealing with each of us. We need to do what we know we are supposed to do and not focus on what others do. We are to obey Christ and love others. We are not called to be the judge of others. That is God's job.

This pretty much sums up the first four verses but also the entire chapter. The chapter lists various ways we tend to judge our brothers. The first four verses discuss the issue of judging another in the way they eat, the way they live their daily lives. James also warns about speaking evil against each other.

> "Do not speak against one another, brethren. He who speaks against a brother or judges his brother, speaks against the law and judges the law; but if you judge the law, you are not a doer of the law but a judge of it."
> (James 4:11)

Warren Wiersbe describes this first-century problem:

> This passage ". . . deals with the problem of questionable things in the Christian life and what to do when sincere Christians disagree about personal practices. Paul recognizes that in each local church there are mature believers ("We that are strong," Ro 15:1) as well as immature ("him that is weak in faith," Ro 14:1) and that these two groups may disagree on how the Christian is to live. The Jewish Christians might want to cling to special holy days and OT dietary laws, while the Gentile believers might turn

Two thousand years after Paul wrote these words, we still struggle with judging others over the way they live. We find fault in the brethren if they do a certain thing or if they don't do a certain thing. We make ourselves the standard by which others are measured. That is clearly wrong. The only standards are those God gives. The only judgments to be made are from God, not us.

Christ is the Master. We are the servant. **Verse 4** reminds us of that. Christ chooses the assignments and duties of the servants. When we judge the work of another servant, we call into question the One who gives the assignments.

Romans 14:5-9 We are not to judge others in regards to religious practices.

5 One person regards one day above another, another regards every day *alike*. Each person must be fully convinced in his own mind. **6** He who observes the day, observes it for the Lord, and he who eats, does so for the Lord, for he gives thanks to God; and he who eats not, for the Lord he does not eat, and gives thanks to God. **7** For not one of us lives for himself, and not one dies for himself; **8** for if we live, we live for the Lord, or if we die, we die for the Lord; therefore, whether we live or die, we are the Lord's. **9** For to this end Christ died and lived again, that He might be Lord both of the dead and of the living.

Christians can also be judgmental about others' religious practices and preferences. Some worship on Sunday, others on

Saturday. Since I became a Christian, I can't tell Saturday from Sunday, or Tuesday from Wednesday. Our walk with Christ is seven days a week. One person rests from his activities on Sunday. The preacher works harder on that day than other days. He might find a day of rest on Monday. Another might have to teach all week and serve on Sunday as well. He has a daily rest in the Lord as a portion of each day. Why should we be troubled if others have different religious practices than we do? If they are children of God, then it is not our assignment to judge them or point out their perceived faults.

The Living New Testament on **Verse 5**:

> **"In the same way, some think one day is more holy than another day, while others think every day is alike. Each person should have a personal conviction about this matter."** (NLT - Tyndale House)

When Bible commentator R.A. Torrey released his book "What the Bible Teaches," he was accused of being arrogant. After all, who can dogmatically say "I know what the Bible teaches." He was publicly challenged about his book title. His response was a good one. He lifted up one of his hard-bound books and pointed out the spine of the book which only had the words "What the Bible Teaches" on the top and the author's name on the bottom, "Torrey." He then said that the book is about "What the Bible teaches Torrey!" Not every believer will believe everything exactly the same. There are big differences between convictions and preferences. We can stand firm on the foundations of the faith, but let us not destroy those in the family of God just because they eat a ham sandwich or worship on a different day than we do.

The main point of **Verse 5** is that we each need to personally follow our conscience. Paul reminded the Colossians about this issue of Christian liberty.

"Therefore let no one act as your judge in regard to food or drink or in respect to a festival or a new moon or a Sabbath day—things which are a mere shadow of what is to come; but the substance belongs to Christ."
(Colossians 2:16, 17)

The mature believer knows he is free from the restraints of days and foods. He also has a measure of grace towards others who may be weaker in their judgments. Those who are personally driven to follow certain other days or restrain from certain foods. The mature believer is fully convinced of his freedom and filled with grace towards those who see things differently within the body of Christ.

CONVICTIONS VS. PREFERENCES

Convictions. The root word is "convinced." A conviction is a belief that a person is fully convinced is true. Some describe convictions as beliefs that are not negotiable. In other words, they will not be changed by any argument or appeal. A person with certain convictions will literally die for those beliefs. Biblical convictions usually mean that some things are right and others are wrong.

Preferences. The dictionary simply says it means to prefer one thing over something else. Preferences are not a matter of right and wrong but more about personal choice. They might be influenced by the Bible, but often they are just a matter of picking what a person wants to do or to have. A church meeting may decide on the color to paint the building, but that should not divide the church. That is a preference. When a conviction is challenged, it is an offense, but when a preference is challenged, it is an irritation. The problem comes when some believers make preferences into convictions. They start adding rules based on what they prefer. How a person dresses for a worship service would normally be considered a preference, but some have legalistically demanded certain dress codes to be considered a true Christian. In **Romans 14**, Paul is dealing with conflict. The Jews had certain rituals they grew up with and expected them to remain in the church while Gentiles had a very different background. Much of **Romans 14** is comparing the two backgrounds of the mature believer and the weaker brother.

Romans 14:10-13 All of our actions against our brethren will be judged by God.

10 But you, why do you judge your brother? Or you again, why do you regard your brother with contempt? For we will all stand before the judgment seat of God. **11** For it is written,

"As I live, says the Lord, every knee shall bow to Me,
And every tongue shall give praise to God."

12 So then each one of us will give an account of himself to God. **13** Therefore let us not judge one another anymore, but rather determine this—not to put an obstacle or a stumbling block in a brother's way.

This section is summarized by **Verse 13**. Paul is concerned about the harm that can come to the body of Christ when mature, or stronger brothers cause weaker brothers to violate their conscience. We have responsibilities before God and will give an account to Christ at the Judgment.

There were mature believers in the church in Rome who had little patience for less mature Christians, even looked at them with disgust. It was an arrogant attitude. Paul reminds them that the death of Christ was for all and in the end, all will confess Jesus Christ is Lord and praise Him. All are important to God, so how can any of us judge or look down on another believer.

Paul is pleading with the Roman church not to go to war with each other. Unity in the body is necessary for the Church to stand strong against their real enemies. Since the Church is the army of God, then we can't be fighting, stumbling and tripping over each other.

Romans 14:14-23 We are not to do anything that causes a believer to stumble.

14 I know and am convinced in the Lord Jesus that nothing is unclean in itself; but to him who thinks anything to be unclean, to him it is unclean. **15** For if because of food your brother is hurt, you are no longer walking according to love. Do not destroy with your food him for whom Christ died. **16** Therefore do not let what is for you a good thing be spoken of as evil; **17** for the kingdom of God is not eating and drinking, but righteousness and peace and joy in the Holy Spirit. **18** For he who in this *way* serves Christ is acceptable to God and approved by men. **19** So then we pursue the things which make for peace and the building up of one another. **20** Do not tear down the work of God for the sake of food. All things indeed are clean, but they are evil for the man who eats and gives offense. **21** It is good not to eat meat or to drink wine, or *to do anything* by which your brother stumbles. **22** The faith which you have, have as your own conviction before God. Happy is he who does not condemn himself in what he approves. **23** But he who doubts is condemned if he eats, because *his eating is* not from faith; and whatever is not from faith is sin.

This section of Romans is not the first time that we hear that God hates it when His people hurt each other. Look at what God said 1,000 years before Paul penned Romans.

> [16]"There are six things which the LORD HATES,
> Yes, seven which are an abomination to Him:
> [17] Haughty eyes, a lying tongue,
> And hands that shed innocent blood,
> [18] A heart that devises wicked plans,
> Feet that run rapidly to evil,
> [19] A false witness who utters lies,
> And one who spreads strife among brothers."
> (Proverbs 6:11-19)

If you were to make a list of seven things that God hates, would you include the last one found in this list in **Proverbs 6**? The list describes the heart of evil men, those who disregard His Law and cause damage to all around them. They are liars, murderers and lustful, wicked people. They run quickly to evil as we see in this passage. The way the Proverb is worded it seems to point out the last one in a special way. It is saying, God has six things He really hates, actually there are seven. Let's not forget the seventh one! And what is that seventh one, the one that completes the list of the wicked and angers God? It is the person who causes strife or discord in the family of God. It is one who damages the body of Christ, causes divisions within His family. God really hates that.

A FOOD FIGHT

We are told that we can actually destroy a fellow believer by being insensitive to their beliefs about what a believer can eat. We can actually destroy a fellow believer over food. How is that possible?

Not every child of God has the same level of conscience over a number of things. They may come from different religious backgrounds or cultural practices. Their traditions may be centuries old and have a strong hold on them. They may not have been taught what it means to have freedom in Christ. They may be very comfortable and feel closer to God on certain days, or festivals, or eating certain foods. If, by pressure or ridicule, they do what the crowd does, and in doing so, they violate their own conscience. They are sinning according to **Verse 23**. We are to blame if we cause that to happen.

Those who are stronger in faith must show restraint, love, and tolerance for the weaker brother. Every believer needs to avoid causing strife in the body of Christ.

I heard a former Muslim share this story. His family was a strong middle Eastern Muslim family. The son came to Christ while studying at a university in America. He always visited his family once a year. While eating one day in the cafeteria at his university, one of his Christian friends said "I notice you never eat ham or pork products. You do know, as Christians, we are free to eat these things." The young man answered, "Yes, I know that. But each year when I go home to visit my family, my father always asks the same thing before he lets me into his house, 'Son, has the filthy hog meat ever touched your lips?' And I tell him, 'No, father, it has not.' Then he lets me into the house."

This converted Muslim was able to use the liberty he had to respect the culture and beliefs of his family. That story, in essence, is what this section of Romans is all about. Considering others above our freedoms.

This theme of denying our own freedoms and choices for the sake of others is continued in **Chapter 15**.

Romans Chapter 15

Setting aside our personal preferences for the sake of the body of Christ

" . . . I urge you, brethren, by our Lord Jesus Christ and by the love of the Spirit, to strive **together** with me . . . "

Romans 15:30

CHAPTER 15 SUMMARY

This chapter is really the end of the letter. **Chapter 16** is basically a list of greetings and accommodations to those who had helped Paul along the way over the years. **Chapter 15** concludes his teachings and exhortations to the Church at Rome, made up of both Jews and Gentiles. He strongly appeals to both groups to live in unity and in the grace of our Lord Jesus Christ. His example is Jesus Himself, who loves every member the Church. Paul then reminds the believers that the Holy Spirit is the one who will give us hope, peace, and power in the ministry. Paul then concludes by recounting his journey of preaching the Gospel to the Gentiles and tells of his plan to visit them in Rome. Finally, he asks for prayer and then prays a final benediction for the Church in Rome.

THE KEY VERSES FOR CHAPTER 15

"[1]Now we who are strong ought to bear the weaknesses of those without strength and not just please ourselves. [2] Each of us is to please his neighbor for his good, to his edification. [3] For even Christ did not please Himself;"

SIMPLE OUTLINE

I. Romans 15:1-6 — Those strong in faith need to build unity in the body and help the weaker brethren.

II. Romans 15:7-12 — The example of Christ who loved both Jews and Gentiles.

III. Romans 15:13-21 — Our hope, peace and power come from the Holy Spirit.

IV. Romans 15:22-29 — Paul recounts his journey and his plan to visit Rome.

V. Romans 15:30-33 — Paul requests prayer for himself and gives his final benediction.

Romans 15 Commentary

THE WEAKER BROTHER

We all know that not every believer is the same. Some have great maturity, others struggle with their faith. Some are older believers while some are new converts. Religious and cultural backgrounds differ greatly, as do different individual temperaments. Believers have different Spiritual Gifts. The body of Christ is represented by different peoples, tribes, tongues, and nations.

Romans 15 is Paul's heart of compassion for those in the body who are weaker in faith, bound by their cultures and religious traditions. He knows some struggle with their consciences, while others celebrate their freedom in Christ. Paul exhorts the believers who are enjoying their freedoms to be sensitive to the members of the body that are bound by their traditions. His concern is that those who are enjoying freedom will put pressure on the weaker brethren to conform to the crowd and violate their conscience. That would cause the weaker brother to sin. It would also be sinful for the one who caused the problem and the tension.

We need to love all members of the body and that means looking out for each other and not doing anything which would cause another to stumble.

Romans 15:1-6. Those strong in faith need to build unity in the body and help the weaker brethren.

1Now we who are strong ought to bear the weaknesses of those without strength and not *just* please ourselves. **2** Each of us is to please his neighbor for his good, to his edification. **3** For even Christ did not please Himself; but as it is written, "THE REPROACHES OF THOSE WHO REPROACHED YOU FELL ON ME." **4** For whatever was written in earlier times was written for our instruction, so that through perseverance and the encouragement of the Scriptures we might have hope. **5** Now may the God who gives perseverance and encouragement grant you to be of the same mind with one another according to Christ Jesus, **6** so that with one accord you may with one voice glorify the God and Father of our Lord Jesus Christ.

The first instruction of **Chapter 15** is a plea for unity in the body of Christ to live unselfish lives. The Roman culture was known for excesses in personal pleasure. Paul's appeal is for believers to focus on others instead of themselves.

Paul contrasts the life of living in a hedonistic (pleasure-seeking) world with being part of God's Kingdom, the world of God. Instead of pursuing personal pleasures, the believer should be seeking the well being of others. The Roman gods were fleshy, self-seeking, and even immoral. God is very different. Our role model is Jesus who gave Himself for others. The Christian life is not about pleasing ourselves but helping our neighbor.

To be able to make that break from the society that attracted them would require a good amount of perseverance and encouragement. The phrase, "perseverance and encouragement," is used in both **Verses 4 and 5**. If the body of Christ works together, the strong helping the weak, we will become of one mind and glorify God (**Verses 5 and 6**)

Romans 15:7-12. The example of Christ who loved both the Jews and the Gentiles.

7 Therefore, accept one another, just as Christ also accepted us to the glory of God. 8 For I say that Christ has become a servant to the circumcision on behalf of the truth of God to confirm the promises *given* to the fathers, 9 and for the Gentiles to glorify God for His mercy; as it is written,

> "THEREFORE I WILL GIVE PRAISE TO YOU AMONG THE GEN-
> TILES,
> AND I WILL SING TO YOUR NAME."

10 Again he says,

> "REJOICE, O GENTILES, WITH HIS PEOPLE."

11 And again,

> "PRAISE THE LORD ALL YOU GENTILES,
> AND LET ALL THE PEOPLES PRAISE HIM."

12 Again Isaiah says,

> "THERE SHALL COME THE ROOT OF JESSE,
> AND HE WHO ARISES TO RULE OVER THE GENTILES,
> IN HIM SHALL THE GENTILES HOPE."

The first six verses show the stronger members and the weaker members of the body are to handle the conflicts that had arisen in the Roman church. All believers, stronger and weaker are to learn to accept one another as equal members of the church.

In **Verses 7-12,** Paul lays out the argument that God has accepted each of us, so we need to do the same. He gives us several Old

Testament passages to prove that this has been the will of God since the beginning.

In **Verse 8,** Paul discusses the Jews. God had given many promises to the nation of Israel. He had given them the Abrahamic and Davidic covenants and instituted circumcision as a sign of His special relationship with His people. When Jesus the Messiah came, He came as a servant to His people.

> **"Just as the Son of Man did not come to be served, but to serve, and to give his life as a ransom for many."**
> (Matthew 20:28)

God, through the centuries, had entrusted His great Messianic program to His chosen people. He communicated His purposes to the "fathers," Moses, Abraham, Isaac, Jacob, and David. This was not just a blessing for the Jewish nation but was also a blessing for the Gentile world. Even though some in Paul's day looked down on the Jewish believers, God is reminding them that they are special to Him.

Verse 9 reminds the Jews that the Gentiles, being grafted into the Jewish rootstock (**Romans 11**), are now His vessels bringing glory to God. The promises God gave Israel are for all believers, whether they are Jew or Gentile. Paul then lists Old Testament Scriptures showing God is true and keeps His promises:

Verse 9 — (Psalm 18:49) *"Therefore I will give thanks to You among the nations, O LORD, And I will sing praises to Your name."* This Psalm promises that the Gentile nations will sing the praises of God because of the promises made to Israel.

Verse 10 — (Deuteronomy 32:43) is partially quoted and promises the same thing. God tells the Gentile nations to rejoice together with the Jewish nation for the privilege of being counted among the protected people of God.

"Rejoice, O nations, with His people;
For He will avenge the blood of His servants,
And will render vengeance on His adversaries,
And will atone for His land *and* His people."

Verse 11 quotes **Psalm 117:1**, and refers to all nations, Jew and Gentile:

"Praise the LORD, ALL NATIONS;
Laud Him, all peoples!"

In **Verse 12.** Paul finishes his Old Testament proofs by referencing **Isaiah 11:10**:

"Then in that day
The nations will resort to the root of Jesse,
Who will stand as a signal for the peoples;
And His resting place will be glorious."

It is clear that the entire body of Christ is exhorted to love each other and give up the prejudices that divide one another. How do we do that? For many who read the letter to the Romans, the prejudices were deeply held for centuries. One thing we know about God is that when He gives a command, He provides the enabling to obey that command. This brings us to the next section.

Romans 15:13-21. Our hope, peace, power, and results come from the Holy Spirit

13 Now may the God of hope fill you with all joy and peace in believing, so that you will abound in hope by the power of the Holy Spirit.

14 And concerning you, my brethren, I myself also am convinced that you yourselves are full of goodness, filled with all knowledge and able also to admonish one another.

15 But I have written very boldly to you on some points so as to remind you again, because of the grace that was given me from God, **16** to be a minister of Christ Jesus to the Gentiles, ministering as a priest the gospel of God, so that *my* offering of the Gentiles may become acceptable, sanctified by the Holy Spirit. **17** Therefore in Christ Jesus I have found reason for boasting in things pertaining to God. **18** For I will not presume to speak of anything except what Christ has accomplished through me, resulting in the obedience of the Gentiles by word and deed, **19** in the power of signs and wonders, in the power of the Spirit; so that from Jerusalem and round about as far as Illyricum I have fully preached the gospel of Christ. **20** And thus I aspired to preach the gospel, not where Christ was *already* named, so that I would not build on another man's foundation; **21** but as it is written,

> "THEY WHO HAD NO NEWS OF HIM SHALL SEE,
> AND THEY WHO HAVE NOT HEARD SHALL UNDERSTAND."

Everything in **Verse 13** is exactly what we need to know. God is a God of hope and wants to fill our lives with all joy and peace. He wants to empower us with the Holy Spirit to enable us to walk victoriously as Christians in a world that is hostile to God.

This is the power and hope the first-century Church needed to overcome the deeply rooted prejudices that existed between the believing Jews and Gentiles. No problem is so deep that God is not deeper.

Verse 14. Paul is saying, "I believe in you. You can do this. You can build each other up and God is going to help you."

Verse 15. The reason Paul is convinced the Church can learn to believe in one another and break the shackles of prejudice is that God helped him to do it. Paul was a Jew's Jew and hated the Church. It was the grace of God that changed his heart from hate to love. He hated the Church, but Christ changed all that. Paul knew God could do the same to the Roman Church.

Paul lists some of the changes God made in his life as proof that God's grace can change the lives of his readers as well.

Verse 16. God chose Paul, the orthodox Pharisee, to become a missionary to the Gentiles, a people he previously resented. In doing so, Paul's life honored God and was blessed with the power of the Holy Spirit to accomplish what would have been impossible for him.

Verse 17. Paul was a very proud Jewish leader. He had a very strong Jewish religious heritage. God broke that pride and now his only boast is in the grace of God.

Verse 18. The things he used to talk about, the matters of Jewish Law, are now seen in a new light, the light of God. As a Christian, Paul has a new message, Christ crucified, and that Gospel is all he proclaims to the Gentiles.

Verse 19. God has authenticated His presence in Paul's life through miraculous signs and wonders. God is the one who has led Paul to regions beyond his comfort zone. God became his travel agent, and everywhere he goes he preaches the full Gospel of Christ.

Verses 20, 21. The heart of Paul has been completely changed by God. He formerly was a man rising in Jewish leadership and esteemed by the Jewish world. Now he has a desire to go where no man has ever taken the Gospel, no matter how difficult it is.

Anyone who knew Paul and read these testimonies about the grace of God would understand that the God of Paul is their God. The same power and grace are available to them to overcome any obstacle or prejudice like Paul had done.

He then concludes his testimony with **Verse 21** which is a quote from **Isaiah 52:15**:

> **"Thus, He will sprinkle many nations,**
> **Kings will shut their mouths on account of Him;**
> **For what had not been told them they will see,**
> **And what they had not heard they will understand."**

Paul uses this verse to show that he and others who take the Gospel to the unreached people of the earth, are part of fulfilling God's Great Commission. The unreached needed to hear so they could understand. This Great Commission is still valid today, because God is still *"not wishing for any to perish but for all to come to repentance."* (**2 Peter 3:9**)

Romans 15:22-29. Paul recounts his journey and his plan to visit Rome.

22 For this reason I have often been prevented from coming to you; **23** but now, with no further place for me in these regions, and since I have had for many years a longing to come to you **24** whenever I go to Spain—for I hope to see you in passing, and to be helped on my way there by you, when I have first enjoyed your company for a while— **25** but now, I am going to Jerusalem serving the saints. **26** For Macedonia and Achaia have been pleased to make a contribution for the poor among the ⌜saints in Jerusalem. **27** Yes, they were pleased *to do so*, and they are indebted to them. For if the Gentiles have shared in their spiritual things, they are indebted to minister to them also in material things. **28** Therefore, when I have finished this, and have put my seal on this fruit of theirs, I will go on by way of you to Spain. **29** I know that when I come to you, I will come in the fullness of the blessing of Christ.

Verse 22. Paul says he had been hindered, or unable, to come to Rome or the western region. The previous verses give the reason why. Paul was busy church planting, traveling, writing and dealing with issues in Corinth, in Greece and Asia Minor. He simply couldn't fit in a trip to Rome.

Verses 23, 24. Paul now feels the time has come to travel again. He has exhausted all the places to plant a new church. He wants to travel as far west as he can. His plan is to go to the uttermost part of the known earth, the land known as Hispania (Spain). It was the most westerly land in the Roman Empire at that time. On the way to Spain, Paul will stop in Rome to rest and minister to the Roman church. He did go to Rome, but apparently never made it to Spain.

Verses 25-27. First, Paul had something to do. A significant financial offering was gathered by the Gentile churches and was to be given to the suffering Jewish Christians in Jerusalem. According to Paul, the Gentiles were aware of the debt they owed the people of Israel who had been the channel God used to send Jesus to the world. They wanted to demonstrate their thanks by helping the Jewish Church in their need.

Verses 28, 29. Once Paul has delivered that gift, he was heading to Rome for that long-desired visit.

Romans 15:30-33 Paul's requests prayer for himself and gives his final benediction

30 Now I urge you, brethren, by our Lord Jesus Christ and by the love of the Spirit, to strive together with me in your prayers to God for me, **31** that I may be rescued from those who are disobedient in Judea, and *that* my service for Jerusalem may prove acceptable to the saints; **32** so that I may come to you in joy by the will of God and find *refreshing* rest in your company. **33** Now the God of peace be with you all. Amen.

Paul concludes his instructions to the Romans with a prayer request for himself. Following this final request, he sends greetings to various co-workers and special friends in **Chapter 16**.

He asks in his prayer that the gift he is carrying to the Jewish church in Jerusalem be received in a manner that will be a blessing to them. His hope is for healing of the problems faced by Jew and Gentile believers.

He asks prayer for a specific group of people in Judea that are troublemakers. He asks prayer for a good and profitable journey to Rome. He wants to be a blessing to the Roman church.

Romans Chapter 16
Greetings to Paul's co-workers

CHAPTER 16 SUMMARY

Paul closes out his epistle with a section of customary greetings and warnings. He names more than 30 people. Most of these are his friends in Rome and believers he worked with in the cities of Corinth and Ephesus. **Romans** was written at the end of Paul's third missionary journey. Over the years of his highly productive travels, Paul had a strong influence in the lives of many Christian leaders across Asia Minor, the Grecian peninsula, and throughout Israel. The sheer size of the list and the quality of the workers is a great testament to the tireless and sacrificial work of the Apostle Paul. The fruit of his labors were widespread.

THE KEY VERSES FOR CHAPTER 16

"¹Now we who are strong ought to bear the weaknesses of those without strength and not just please ourselves. ² Each of us is to please his neighbor for his good, to his edification. ³ For even Christ did not please Himself;"

SIMPLE OUTLINE

Romans 16:1-16 — General greetings to Paul's co-workers.

Romans 16:17-20 — Warnings about those who divide and deceive.

Romans 16:21-24 — Greetings to the Church in Rome from the believers in Corinth.

Romans 16 Commentary

PHOEBE

In **Romans 16:1, 2** we are introduced to an amazing woman. She was a deaconess, a servant of the church, which probably met in her home. She was a wealthy woman who used her resources to help others. She lived in the eastern seaport of Corinth, a town called Cenchrea. Paul <u>sends greetings</u> to over 30 co-workers in **Romans 16** <u>but he commended</u> Phoebe to the church at Rome. Most scholars recognize that Phoebe was such a dependable worker for God that Paul entrusted his precious manuscript to her keeping. We can conclude from the Greek words used in these two verses that Phoebe was probably a single, wealthy, Greek businesswoman who along with Aquila and Priscilla helped support Paul. Her name was derived from Greek mythology. We can assume she came from a pagan background, but once saved she became one of Paul's most trusted co-workers. Truly, she was one of the great women in the Bible. She is the first person mentioned in Paul's greetings.

Romans 16:1-16.
General greetings to Paul's co-workers

Rather than go into detail about every name in this list, here are some general observations about these first sixteen verses. This is a very special list (Please read it in your Bible). In the first sixteen verses, Paul addresses 29 people. He sends greetings to the various believers in different house Churches. He also greets some without giving a name. There are many detailed commentaries today which go through the names in **Romans 16** in detail. I highly recommend reading about these that Paul recognizes as trusted co-workers.

FROM PAGANS TO CHRISTIAN LEADERS

Many of them came from pagan Greek and Roman backgrounds. Some were named after false Greek gods. Some had been with Paul during times of imprisonment and suffering. Some were traveling companions, some ministry co-workers in church planting. Some helped with financial support, others comforted Paul. Overall, each person listed is seen by Paul as his dream team, his family, his most trusted friends. They are all beloved members of the body of Christ, they were "in Christ."

One can imagine the smile on Paul's face as he looked over the list. What grace God had given to Paul to have such a special, dedicated team of co-workers and friends. They were his joy and he loved them like a father would his children.

IT WASN'T JUST MEN.

In the male-dominated first century world, it is significant that Paul mentions ten women in these verses. He speaks of them with great affection. They helped him at important times in his life. He refers to them as sisters, and one of them he affectionately calls his mother. They supported him emotionally, financially and encouraged him.

Priscilla, a special mention. Priscilla and her husband, Aquila, were Roman citizens. Because they were believers, they were expelled by Emperor Claudius. They would later travel back to Rome when Claudius died, and Nero lifted the ban.

Meanwhile, Priscilla and Aquila traveled to Corinth, where they set up a tent-making business. It is there they met the Apostle

Paul on his second missionary journey. He was drawn to them not just because they were strong Christians, but they also worked in the same trade. He was trained during his rabbinic schooling to make tents from animal skins.

They became one of Paul's most trusted couples. They traveled frequently from Corinth to Ephesus where they worked along with Paul and young Timothy in that amazing church plant. Priscilla and Aquila helped disciple an Alexandrian Jew from Egypt, Apollos. He later became a powerful evangelist and apologist traveling throughout Asia Minor and Greece. Paul lists them at the top of the list of greetings. They were definitely on Paul's A-list.

Romans 16: 17-20.
Warnings about those who divide and deceive.

17 Now I urge you, brethren, keep your eye on those who cause dissensions and hindrances contrary to the teaching which you learned, and turn away from them. 18 For such men are slaves, not of our Lord Christ but of their own appetites; and by their smooth and flattering speech they deceive the hearts of the unsuspecting. 19 For the report of your obedience has reached to all; therefore, I am rejoicing over you, but I want you to be wise in what is good and innocent in what is evil. 20 The God of peace will soon crush Satan under your feet. The grace of our Lord Jesus be with you.

When Paul finished his three years establishing the Church in

Ephesus, he warned the believers about false teachers who, like vicious wild animals, would descend on the Church to devour it.

> **"I know that after my departure savage wolves will come in among you, not sparing the flock."** (Acts 20:29)

His final words to the church in Rome were to be on the alert against people within the church who teach doctrines contrary to the truth they had been taught from the beginning. **Verse 17** teaches that these people cause fighting within the church and harm the testimony of the local church. **Verse 20** puts the spotlight on the source of the problems, Satan himself, and one day the final destruction of our enemy is coming. Paul was a good shepherd, providing good food for the flocks of God and protection against the wolves that would destroy and scatter the flocks. These people had caused Paul much personal grief. Jesus had warned that people like this would be among us **(Matthew 24:24).**

Romans 16:21-24.
Greetings to the Church in Rome from the believers in Corinth

21 Timothy my fellow worker greets you, and *so do* Lucius and Jason and Sosipater, my kinsmen.

22 I, Tertius, who write this letter, greet you in the Lord.

23 Gaius, host to me and to the whole church, greets you. Erastus, the city treasurer greets you, and Quartus, the brother. **24** [The grace of our Lord Jesus Christ be with you all. Amen.]

25 Now to Him who is able to establish you according to my gospel and the preaching of Jesus Christ, according to the revelation of the mystery which has been kept secret for long ages past, **26** but now is manifested, and by the Scriptures of the prophets, according to the commandment of the eternal God, has been made known to all the nations, *leading* to obedience of faith; **27** to the only wise God, through Jesus Christ, be the glory forever. Amen.

Paul concludes with special greetings from various believers in Corinth. He begins with the person he had become closest to over the years. It was as close as a father/son relationship. He was Paul's most faithful fellow-worker, Timothy.

In **Verse 22**, a very interesting person is mentioned, Tertius. Tertius was Paul's secretary in Corinth. Some believe he was a former slave.

Another interesting inclusion is found in **Verse 23**. Erastus, the city treasurer, is a very high government official who follows Christ. An actual first-century inscription has been found in Corinth that identifies Erastus as a top government official. Luke lists both Timothy and Erastus as key co-workers.

> [22] **"And having sent into Macedonia two of those who ministered to him, Timothy and Erastus, he himself stayed in Asia for a while."** (Acts 19:22)

Paul mentions Erastus when he writes his final letter to Timothy. Here are some verses from the final words of Paul:

> [19] **"Greet Prisca and Aquila, and the household of Onesiphorus.** [20] **Erastus remained at Corinth, but Trophimus I left sick at Miletus."** (2 Timothy 4:19, 20)

From everything we can tell, Erastus was one of the earliest evangelists to bring the Gospel to the Gentile world. He was a close companion of Paul.

In these final greetings, we find everyone from converted slaves to a top Roman government official. They had been converted and became ministers of the Gospel to the lost world. It is a picture of grace that they each worked together without social status being an issue.

With that thought, Paul closes his Epistle.

PERSONAL THOUGHTS ON OUR JOURNEY THROUGH ROMANS.

After writing this, I have come to appreciate the Apostle Paul more than at any previous time. His intellect was unmatched. He stood before the wisest philosophers in the world in Athens. His knowledge of the Old Testament was deep having been a Pharisee in the Jewish discipline and having spent three years in Arabia in Jesus' school of Truth. He had the most complete knowledge of God and the Scriptures of any man on the earth at that time. He suffered as much as any man for his faith and through it all, his faith in Christ was enough.

He mingled with kings and slaves. Through it all, he treated them equally. They were people that needed Jesus. He spoke with great power and humility. He traveled much of the known world, planting Churches in different regions of the world, while writing half of the New Testament and discipling the believers. He finished well, with a note of victory. Romans is the final masterpiece of the totality of Paul's life.

Paul was a trophy of the God's grace. A man who previously focused on destroying the Church, now transformed into a man God used to plant and grow the Church. All his greetings and writing credit the grace of God. To Paul, it was all about grace.

Amen and Amen!

Made in the USA
Monee, IL
10 March 2022

92647008R00173